AF595825

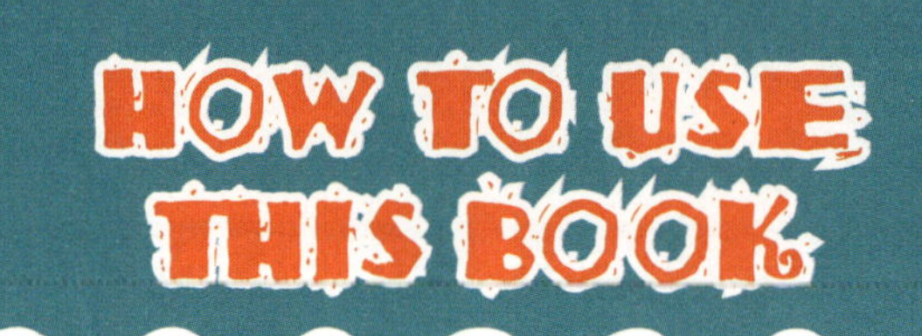

General Capabilities form one dimension of the Australian Curriculum, the others being the Learning Areas and the Cross-Curriculum Priorities. General Capabilities are taught through the content of the Learning Areas and involve knowledge, skills, behaviour and dispositions.

There are seven General Capabilities, and this *Targeting General Capabilities* Assessment book examines two of them: Critical and Creative Thinking, and Ethical Understanding. The two General Capabilities are further divided into their elements: seven in all. Each unit begins with a stimulus, followed by assessable activities that examine the element through the different Learning Areas. The table below provides a quick page reference to the different Learning Areas examined via each General Capability element in this book. You will find the relevant links to the Australian Curriculum at the beginning of each section.

Unit	Elements	English	HASS	HPE	Maths	Science	Tech	The Arts
Critical and Creative Thinking								
1	Inquiring, exploring and organising information and ideas	4			6	8		
2	Generating ideas, possibilities and actions	12, 14	10, 13					15
3	Reflecting on thinking and processes	16	18		21	20		
4	Analysing, synthesising and evaluating reasoning and procedures	22	26		24			
Ethical Understanding								
5	Understanding ethical concepts and issues	39, 42		37, 38		39		
6	Reasoning in decision-making and actions	43		45	47			43
7	Exploring values, rights and responsibilities	49	51	52			54	

On the last page of each unit, space is allocated for self-reflection. Students have the opportunity to explore what they have learnt about each element and to record their thoughts.

There is an assessment section at the end of each General Capability where tasks are tailored to the sub-elements, rather than through the lens of a specific Learning Area. This consolidates students' understanding of the concepts and provides guidance for further reflection.

Critical & Creative Thinking

Through developing Critical and Creative Thinking Capability, children learn to generate and evaluate knowledge, clarify concepts and ideas, seek possibilities, consider alternatives and solve problems. As outlined in the curriculum, the elements and sub-elements are:

Inquiring, exploring and organising information and ideas — pose questions; identify and clarify information and ideas; organise and process information

Generating ideas, possibilities and actions — imagine possibilities and connect ideas; consider alternatives; seek solutions and put ideas into action

Reflecting on thinking and processes — think about thinking (metacognition); reflect on processes; transfer knowledge into new contexts

Analysing, synthesising and evaluating reasoning and procedures — apply logic and reasoning; draw conclusions and design a course of action; evaluate procedures and outcomes

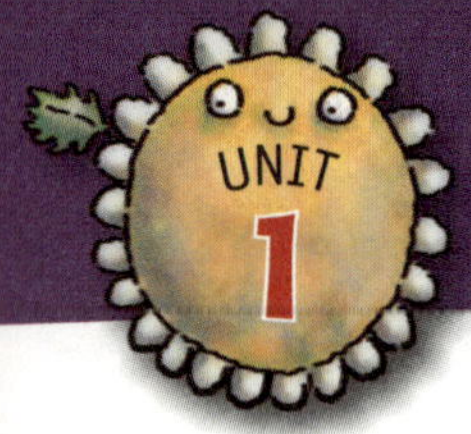

Inquiring

English – Literacy & Literature

Australian Curriculum Links: *Year 5 ACELY1702, ACELT1608 / Year 6 ACELY1801, ACELT1613*

CRITICAL & CREATIVE THINKING

MURDER

I snuck up on him ever so quietly. I could see his chest rise and fall with the evenness of his breathing, his eyes closed and his head resting on the sack he used as a pillow. I had the weapon concealed in my mouth, razor sharp and ready to use. Carefully, I wound my way around the other forms in the room, all breathing quietly and rhythmically in the dark, their silhouettes just visible in the gloom and their beds packed close together. In one lunge I grabbed him and used the weapon in my mouth.

Unfortunately, I had slipped on the side of the bed and only managed to wound him. He shrieked and fought against me, but my grip was too strong. The others were alerted to my presence and set up such a din that I knew I would be apprehended if I did not drag him away from his wives, away from the lights that were blinking to life. His body fell limp in my grip, and I knew he would struggle no more. However, his weight and bulk were difficult to manoeuvre through the fences and out into the woods where I knew I would have a better chance of escape.

I could hear the dogs. They were after me. I thought of my own wife and children, curled up together, safe underground. The baying of the dogs was getting closer, and regretfully I had to let the body go—it was slowing me down. Then I felt it, a searing pain through my leg, and I knew I had been shot. I limped on, the dogs growing closer and the flashlights appearing through the trees. I could go no further, and when the dogs and men caught up with me, I saw the rifle levelled at my head.

'Blasted fox! He took the rooster this time. I don't know how many chickens I've lost to them.'

'I know, Dad, at least we got this one. Can I have the tail? It will look good in my car.'

With that, the farmer and his son collected the body of the fox. Meanwhile, a family waited underground, safe.

1. The first part of the story is from the perspective of …

   a) a farmer. b) a criminal. c) a fox. d) a chicken.

2. What was the weapon held in the murderer's mouth?

   ____

3. Look back at the story, Murder. Now that you know the identity of the narrator at the start of the story, find three pieces of information that provide clues to their identity.

   i. ______________________________

   ii. ______________________________

   iii. ______________________________

4. What is another word for 'manoeuvre'?

   a) eat b) manipulate c) kill d) manhandle

TARGETING GENERAL CAPABILITIES: CRITICAL & CREATIVE THINKING AND ETHICAL UNDERSTANDING YEARS 5-6 © PASCAL PRESS ISBN: 978-1-925726-251

TO CATCH A THIEF

I waited for the phone call. It would not take long. There was another robbery at the jewellery store. Another smashed window and discarded empty boxes, and the press waiting for news of the investigation. I walked in and put on the gloves offered to me. I walked around the crime scene examining the police photographs—I was already familiar with how it looked. I watched as the forensic squad dusted for fingerprints and looked for evidence. I knew there would be no evidence to find. Whoever was the culprit, they were a professional, leaving no prints, no evidence. It was the fourth jewellery store in as many weeks and only the best diamonds were taken. I was being pressured by my supervisors to catch the thief. There was also pressure from the store owners and of course the press, demanding that we catch the culprit. If only I had a suspect.

I arrived home late, again. Another heated dinner in the microwave while I waited for the next phone call. I knew it would come. While I waited for my meal to heat and the phone to ring, I tried on one last bracelet. I watched as the light reflected in the many facets of the stone. I marvelled at its beauty. With great care, I placed it in the safe with the others and replaced the floorboard. Then, I heard the phone ring.

5 What profession is the narrator?

a) police officer b) cleaner c) photographer d) reporter

6 Why was the scene of the crime already familiar to the narrator?

___

7 Why did the narrator have a bracelet, and what was the stone being described: 'light reflected in the many facets'?

___

___

8 Why would the phone ring at the end of the story?

___

___

Your view

9 A plot twist is a story that has an ending that readers do not expect in which either something shocking happens or something shocking is revealed. The storyteller will set up expectations and then twist those expectations by revealing new information.

In a notebook or on your device, write your own short story with a twist at the end. Remember to give small clues in the story that only make sense once the whole story is read.

CRITICAL & CREATIVE THINKING

UNIT 1

Mathematics – Measurement & Geometry

Australian Curriculum Links: *Year 5 ACMMG110, ACMMG108 / Year 6 ACMMG139, ACMMG136*

ON SAFARI IN AFRICA

You have won an all-expenses paid, 10 days/9 nights African Safari Experiences holiday! You will be travelling in small planes and space is very limited. You can only pack a maximum of 12 kg of clothing and toiletries in the African Safari Experiences duffle bag provided to ensure it fits in the plane's hold.

African Safari Experiences has provided a list of things you should take with you and has indicated an approximate weight for each item.

You must select no more than 12 kg of clothing including toiletries from this list. Make sure you don't forget to include the items marked with an * as they will be very important on your Safari. Pack for cool nights and warm days.

Item	Qty	Weight	Total Weight	Item	Qty	Weight	Total Weight
*Sunhat		1.5 kg		*Long-sleeved shirts – lightweight		500 g ea	
*Underwear		0.500 kg ea		*Long pants – lightweight		1.75 kg ea	
*T-Shirts – cotton		0.5 kg ea		*Insect repellent – roll-on/atomiser/ lotion (not aerosol cans)		0.500 kg	
Pyjamas – lightweight		1.5 kg					
*Rain jacket – lightweight		750 g		*Toilet bag with toothbrush, toothpaste, soap, brush/comb		1.5kg	
*Small towel – quick dry type		0.75 kg					
*Sturdy walking boots		2.5 kg		Personal item/s – book, camera, notepad, sketchpad, pens, drawing pencils (Item/s selected must not weigh more than 1 kg in total.)		1 kg	
Covered shoes – lightweight		1.0 kg					
*Thick socks – woollen or cotton		0.500 kg pair					
Thongs		500 g pair					
Jacket – lightweight		2.0 kg		*African Safari Experiences Duffle Bag	1	1.5 kg	
Swimmers		1.0 kg		**Total Weight of Packed Bag**			

To prepare for your African Safari Experiences holiday, let's find out some information about a few of the animals you might meet there.

i. On the graph below are drawings of various animals. Work out the approximate height of each animal (measured to the top of their head) and write the answer under each drawing.

ii. Draw yourself onto the graph showing your height.

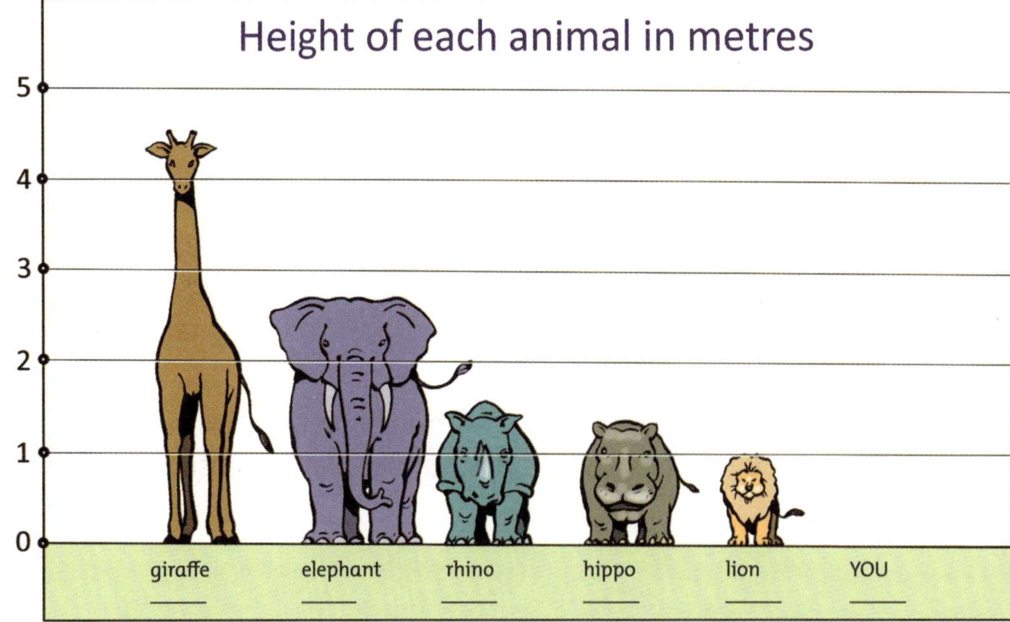

CRITICAL & CREATIVE THINKING

TARGETING GENERAL CAPABILITIES: CRITICAL & CREATIVE THINKING AND ETHICAL UNDERSTANDING YEARS 5-6 © PASCAL PRESS ISBN: 978-1-925726-251

3 As a prize winner, all your accommodation, airfares and meals will be paid for on your African Safari Experiences holiday. However, there are some 'Extras'—activities that you can buy to make your holiday even more special. You have managed to save $100 to take with you for those extra expenses.

African Safari Experience – 'Extras' Brochure

Birds in Flight Exhibition – Daily: 11:00 am–11:30 am **Cost: $5.00**

Getting to Know the Giraffes – Mon & Fri: 09:45–10:45 **Cost: $25.00**

Photo with Baby Monkeys – Mon: 13:00–14:00 **Cost: $30**

African Jungle Nights Tour – Tue & Thurs: 4:30 pm–8:00 pm **Cost: $15.00**

Painting with the Elephants – Wednesday: 1 pm–2 pm **Cost: $30.00**

Feed the Lions – Thurs & Sat: 12:00–16:30 **Cost: $50.00**

Treetops Walk & Zip-line – Thurs & Sun: 12 pm–4:30 pm **Cost: $55.00**

Ranger Talks – Daily: 09:15–10:15 am **Free**

Laze by the pool – Daily: **Free**

All tours start at the main Camp Office 15 minutes before each activity/ tour departure time. Be aware that finishing times are approximate and activities/tours may run over time.

Plan your African Safari experiences itinerary. Refer to the 'Extras' Brochure above for days, times and costs. Write the activities you have decided to do in the table below. Remember, allow time to be able to meet at the Camp Office 15 minutes before each of your planned activities.

	Tues	Wed	Thurs	Fri	Sat	Sun	Mon	Tues	Wed	Thurs
09.00										
9:30										
10:00										
10:30										
11:00										
11:30										
12:00										
12:30										
1:00										
1:30										
14.00	Arrive									Depart
2:30										
3pm										
3:30										
4:00										
4:30										
17.00 onwards										
Cost										
Total Cost of all activities is:										

CRITICAL & CREATIVE THINKING

Science – Science as a Human Endeavour

Australian Curriculum Links: *Years 5 & 6 ACSHE081, ACSHE098, ACSHE083, ACSHE100*

SCENE OF CRIME EVIDENCE – THE CLOTHES IN THE BIN

The items of clothing shown below were found in a rubbish bin on the corner of Welsh and Webster Streets, Oldtown, approximately 500 metres down the street from a crime scene. It is not known if they belong to the perpetrators of the crime or were dumped by some other person.

The Witness Statements as reported to the police are:

Witness 1: I was walking down Welsh Street on my way to the Deli on Webster Street when a person on a motorbike going in the opposite direction whizzed past me and threw a black, plastic garbage bag into the gutter. I was nearly hit by the bag, and I yelled at the bike rider, but the bike didn't stop!

Witness 2: Just as I turned the corner from the Deli on Webster Street, I saw a black garbage bag lying in the gutter. It was open, so I had a look and saw a brown jacket with a dark stain on the left elbow, a pair of jeans with a tear in the back pocket and a Lacoste branded polo shirt. The items were no good to me as I'd never fit into them, so I threw them in the nearest rubbish bin.

Witness 3: A customer had just left when suddenly the front door crashed open and a person wearing a motorbike helmet and a brown jacket demanded money from the cash register. As I was pushed out of the way, the robber knocked my chocolate cake display with their elbow. I was told to put the money in a black, plastic garbage bag. I handed it over and the person took off and jumped on a bike parked outside.

CRITICAL & CREATIVE THINKING

As Chief Crime Scene Investigator (CSI), you have to investigate and sort out all the facts of the case to solve the crime and find the perpetrator.

1. Draw a map of the crime scene area showing where all three Witnesses say they were in their Witness Statements.

TARGETING GENERAL CAPABILITIES: CRITICAL & CREATIVE THINKING AND ETHICAL UNDERSTANDING YEARS 5-6 © PASCAL PRESS ISBN: 978-1-925726-251

UNIT 1

2 Each article of clothing from the black garbage bag has to be identified by using an Evidence Tag. As a Crime Scene Investigator, you need to examine each piece of the clothing and read the Witness Statements to fill in the Evidence Tags. The Evidence Tag for Item #A332 has been completed for you.

Evidence Tag
Item #A332

Evidence Tag
Item #B333

Evidence Tag
Item #C334

Evidence Tag Item #A332	Evidence Tag Item #B333	Evidence Tag Item #C334
Description: Man's brown jacket – purple lining	______________	______________
Stains/Markings/Brand: chocolate stain on left elbow	______________	______________
Location: found in rubbish bin on cnr of Welsh and Webster St, Oldtown	______________	______________

3 After examining the clothing, complete the Forensic Report by filling in the missing words from the list.

Word Bank

Repairs alibi clothing interviewed Analysis
receipt jacket inquiries microscopic male chocolate

________ of the ________ revealed the following:

- brown ________ – the stain on the left elbow proved to be ________ icing
- blue t-shirt – ________ examination of hairs on the collar found them to be from a ________
- blue jeans – a ________ from Milson's Motorcycle ________ was found in the right pocket. The name on the receipt was Chris Robinhood and a phone number was listed.

When ________, Mr Robinhood was not able to provide an ________ for the time of the robbery at the store. Mr Robinhood continues to help us with our ________.

4 After examining all the evidence, including the Witness Statements and the Forensic Report, do you believe that Chris Robinhood committed the crime? What evidence points to him being the robber?

____

____

CRITICAL & CREATIVE THINKING

Generating ideas

HASS – History

Australian Curriculum Links: *Year 5 ACHASSK106, ACHASSK107 / Year 6 ACHASSK137*

PERTH MIRROR

Australia's Last Living Convict

July 1938

Samuel Speed, Australia's last living convict, will turn 97 this year. He was transported to Western Australia in 1866 at the age of 25 where he became an exemplary citizen.

Samuel Speed is the last survivor of the men who were transported to the Swan River Colony as convicts. He was transported for a sentence of seven years for setting fire to a haystack. On questioning, he said he lit the fire to be arrested as he was starving and had no place to sleep in the harsh winter weather.

Samuel Speed was born in Birmingham in 1841 and when sentenced, left behind a sister and a brother, whom he never saw or heard of again. He landed at Fremantle in 1866 aboard the troopship, Belgravia.

Due to his good behaviour and willingness to work, he was released as a bonds man after three years. He has never been re-convicted of any offence and has lived a perfectly ordinary and law-abiding life. He has been held up as an example that the system of transportation worked. It was a system that took corrupt British convicts and turned them into productive members of society.

Although he is old and frail, with a failing memory, he is very much aware of the vast changes that have occurred in his lifetime. He now resides in the Old Men's Home in Perth.

On my visit with Samuel Speed, I asked him several questions ...

Source: https://www.abc.net.au/news/2018-01-10/australias-last-convicts/9317172

CRITICAL & CREATIVE THINKING

 1. When was this story written? ______________________

 2. Why would Samuel Speed want to be arrested?

a) He knew he had done the wrong thing by lighting a fire.

b) He thought prison would be better than being outside in winter.

c) He wanted to be transported to somewhere warmer.

 3. You are a reporter for the Mirror and you have to complete the article. Write three questions you would like to ask Samuel Speed, questions that you and your readers would like to know.

____

____

____

 4. Other words for 'exemplary' could be ...

a) praiseworthy. b) punished and made an example of. c) unknown and forgotten.

 5. Why was Samuel Speed important for transportation?

a) He proved that you can't change people.

b) He proved that people could live long lives in Australia.

c) He proved that convicts could become productive members of society.

TARGETING GENERAL CAPABILITIES: CRITICAL & CREATIVE THINKING AND ETHICAL UNDERSTANDING YEARS 5-6 © PASCAL PRESS ISBN: 978-1-925726-251

Generating ideas

JOHN HUDSON

John Hudson was the youngest convict to be sent to Australia. He was one of 34 children in the First Fleet, arriving in Australia in 1788.

John was born in 1774 as an orphan. He was unable to read or write and spent his life on the streets of London, becoming a chimneysweep where he would climb the inside of chimneys and brush away all the black dust.

Artist impression – A Chimneysweeper (Phillip Lock)

In 1783, at the age of nine, John was charged with breaking and entering into a London house with a friend where they stole one shirt, five silk stockings, one pistol and two aprons. At his trial he had no-one to defend him, and he spoke only 13 words. Luckily, John did not receive the death sentence but instead he was sentenced to seven years transportation. The judge reportedly felt there was a lack of evidence but did not want to release John. He believed he was doing the right thing in sentencing John in order to take him away from people who might be using him. These people used children to rob houses, setting them on a course of a life of crime.

It took four years before John was sent to Australia. During that time, he lived aboard a number of prison ships. He left for Australia in 1787 and arrived on Australian shores the following year at the age of 13.

John was sent to Norfolk Island. The settlement later became notorious for cruelty. This included John receiving '50 lashes for being outside his hut' after 9 pm. His name has not been found on any records after 1795, so it remains a mystery as to what happened to him.

It is recorded that a John Hudson died in 1795 at the age of 20.

Source: https://firstfleetfellowship.org.au/wp-content/uploads/2015/10/from-phillip.jpg

CRITICAL & CREATIVE THINKING

6. If John Hudson had committed these crimes today, what consequences would you consider as appropriate for him to complete and why?

____

____

7. Why do you think John only spoke 13 words?

____

____

8. Why did the judge sentence him to transportation?

a) To get John away from people who would use him to rob houses.

b) To make an example of him for other children to see.

c) To boost the number of children to send to Australia.

d) To punish him for not speaking up in his trial.

What if?

9. What if John Hudson had met Samuel Speed in Australia? What advice could he give John to be successful in his new life in Australia? Write it in the speech bubble provided.

  ISBN: 978-1-925726-251

Generating ideas

English – Literacy

Australian Curriculum Links: *Year 5 ACELY1704 / Year 6 ACELY1714*

1. Re-read the story of John Hudson on page 11.

What if you could rewrite history and the next time you searched online for information about his life, you found a page that told a different story—a story of success and accomplishment?

Rewrite John's experiences in Australia so that he had a long and successful life. Outline what he did in his life and whether he became prosperous, had a family or was a well-known and valued member of society. Start the story when he arrived in Australia at the age of 13.

Present this as a page of information you have found online. Add photographs, pictures, maps or any other visual material to make your page more interesting. You can write your story of John Hudson's life on paper or use your device to create a digital version.

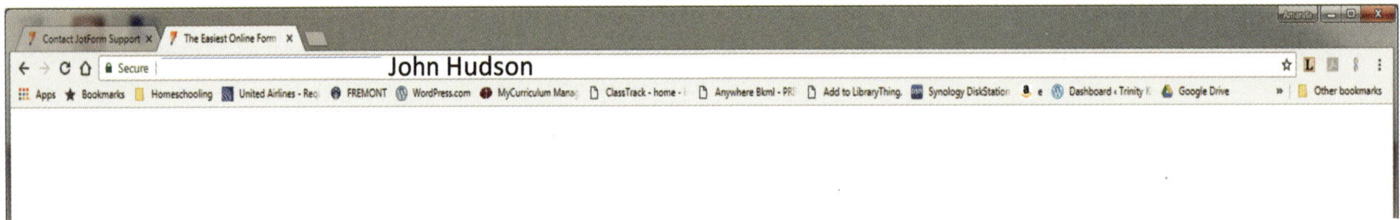

2. Just like young people today, convicts had their own language called 'Flash' language, for example, 'bad', which referred to a convict who cooperated with the police.

Investigate other convict 'Flash' words using this website: https://sydneylivingmuseums.com.au/convict-sydney/flash-language.

Now it's your turn to make up three 'Flash' words you could add to the list and provide a meaning for each word.

Convict 'Flash' Language	Meaning
bad	*a convict who cooperated with the police*

CRITICAL & CREATIVE THINKING

HASS – History

Australian Curriculum Links: *Year 5 ACHASSK110 / Year 6 ACHASSK135*

CLAIM TO FAME

You are organising a party for a group of famous Australians. You've been asked to introduce these famous people to the guests at the party. The problem is no-one has a name tag on, and you don't know who anyone is!

To make matters worse, the information you have been handed to help you introduce each famous guest is all mixed up!

Match up the name of the famous Australian with the reason why they are famous by drawing a line from the name to the description of their 'claim to fame'.

FAMOUS AUSTRALIAN	CLAIM TO FAME
1 Fred Hollows – Ophthalmologist	**A** Between 1967 and 1978, he researched and developed the cochlear implant to enable deaf people to hear other people speak. The cochlear implant is sometimes called a bionic ear. In 1978, the first cochlear implant surgery was successfully completed.
2 Andy Thomas – Aerospace Engineer & Astronaut	**B** She was honoured as Australian of the Year in 2005 after inventing and successfully using 'spray-on skin' to treat patients with serious burns. Using this world-first invention, she and her team were able to save many lives.
3 Kathy Freeman – Olympic Athlete	**C** Born in 1861 in Geraldton, Western Australia, she successfully campaigned for women to have the right to vote. At the age of 59, she was the first woman elected to the Australian Parliament. She is considered one of the most famous Australians in history and is honoured by having her portrait on the $50 note.
4 Professor Graeme Clark – Otolaryngologist	**D** He is a three-time Paralympic gold medallist who has won over 40 marathons as a wheelchair racer. He is also a television and radio host, and inspirational speaker.
5 Dr Fiona Wood – Burns Specialist	**E** Born in 1872, he was a writer and inventor, and stood up for the rights of Aboriginal people. He developed a number of inventions and became known as 'Australia's Leonardo' (da Vinci) because of his passion for scientific ideas. He was the first Aboriginal author to be published, and his face can be seen on the $50 note.
6 Kurt Fearnley – Paralympian	**F** She is the first Aboriginal person to compete in the Olympics, and she lit the Sydney 2000 Olympic flame. She is considered to be Australia's most successful track athlete since Rayleen Boyle. Between 1990 and 2003, she won gold medals at the Commonwealth and Olympic Games in 200 and 400 metre races.
7 Edith Cowan – Australian Parliamentarian	**G** In the 1970s, he helped launch a national program to attack eye disease in Aboriginal Australians. In three years, his team travelled all over outback Australia, treating 30,000 people, performing a thousand operations and prescribing more than 10,000 pairs of glasses.
8 David Unaipon – Inventor and Author	**H** This Adelaide-born Australian-American flew four missions over twelve years (between 1996 and 2005), spending a total of six months in space. He is Australia's first member of NASA's elite astronaut corps.

English – Literacy

Australian Curriculum Links: *Year 5 ACELY1704 / Year 6 ACELY1714*

What if YOU became a famous Australian?

It is the year 2050 and you are now a famous Australian! You are writing your biographical blog for release to the world's media. To help you write your biography, your publishers, *World FameRUs,* have provided you with a list of questions that will guide your writing.

Your publishers have advised you to keep your answers brief—no more than three lines for each question.

1. What are you famous for—in what area of expertise?

____

____

____

2. When did you become famous?

____

____

____

3. How did you become famous?

____

____

____

4. Who, if anyone, benefits from your fame?

____

____

____

5. What advice do you have for children who want to be famous like you?

____

____

____

6. In five words only, describe the type of person you are.

____

The Arts – Visual & Media Arts

Australian Curriculum Links: *Years 5 & 6 ACAVAM114, ACAVAM115, ACAMAM062*

What if you 'branded' your fame?

1. Now that you are famous, the Reserve Bank of Australia wants to honour you by putting your face on the new $500 note. The designers of the notes have asked you to provide a draft of what you would like the note to look like. In the space below, draw a picture of the side of the Australian $500 note showing your face and any design you think represents your fame.

$500

2. Design a logo for your Biographical Blog, incorporating a motto or quote you are famous for, for example, Nike's 'Just do it!' or Toyota's 'Oh, what a feeling!'

3. You are Australian of the Year 2050, and you are so popular that street artists have started to honour you in graffiti art. Draw some street art you would see on a building near your office.

English – Language

Australian Curriculum Links: *Year 5 ACELA1502, ACELA1504, ACELA1512 / Year 6 ACELA1517, ACELA1518, ACELA1525*

CHOCOLATE MINES ARE RUNNING LOW

The world's chocolate mines are running dangerously low, according to new figures published in the latest journal of *World of Desserts*.

The latest crisis to hit our planet is the predicted shortage of chocolate, which will start to impact around Christmas time this year. According to Dr Hershey, who is a leading expert in the mining of chocolate, 'We have enough supplies until Christmas and then mine closures will start to impact on the supply of chocolate for the world's consumers'.

Richard Brown, a chocolate miner of 20 years, says that all chocolate mines will be exhausted in three years. He said, 'This is a problem that will not go away unless scientists come up with an alternative product. The mines in Switzerland are already closing and the largest mine in the US is already closed'. Over three hundred chocolate mines worldwide have been forced to cease operations in the past decade, and 99% of raw chocolate has already been mined, experts warn.

Scientists around the world are working towards creating a substitute, but according to Eaton Barr, head scientist at the Cadbury company, it is difficult to create the texture and taste of this delicious substance.

The price of chocolate has already risen due to the shortage, and some people are starting to stockpile supplies. Irma Gutz, a member of the Chocoholics Anonymous group, has warned that members could become desperate unless a solution to the problem is found.

The world is in danger of running out of mined chocolate and the tradition of Easter may soon become a memory of the past.

Reporter, Ann Hershey

Fake news is false information. False information is sometimes written into news stories to purposely trick you. Usually, these stories are created to either influence people's views or cause confusion. False information can easily deceive people because it might look like a trusted website or use similar names and web addresses to news sites and organisations that you trust. The above story is false information. Did you suspect something was not right?

Read the article and then answer the following questions.

1. This news article is an example of …

a) good news reporting.
b) Ann Hershey's work.
c) alarming news.
d) false information.

2. If you believed this article to be true, this would mean that …

a) chocolate is in danger of running out.
b) chocolate comes from mines.
c) there is a group called Chocoholics Anonymous.
d) all of the above.

Your turn

3 Write your own news article about some fake news that could be mistaken for real information. Write it in the space provided or on your device. Make it look like a newspaper report with a heading and any pictures you would like to include.

HASS – History & Geography

Australian Curriculum Links: *Year 5 ACHASSK107, ACHASSK112, ACHASSK113 / Year 6 ACHASSK135*

GOLD IN THEM THERE HILLS!!!!!

History is full of stories—they tell us what life was like in the past. Many of the stories are told from one perspective or point of view, so it is important that you try to find out how other people may have felt about the same event or time in history.

This is an extract from Bob Smith's diary. Bob was working on a small property with his wife and four children in Victoria, Australia, when gold was discovered in Ballarat, Victoria. Read his description of events.

1852

June 2nd – Heard news that gold had been discovered in Ballarat, in the colony of Victoria. Thought about going, but I'm worried about leaving the wife and kids. I know Jock McKenzie on the next farm is going, should I go?

June 3rd – I've decided, I'm going. I'm going to make our fortune on the goldfields. I leave tomorrow, but the wife isn't happy about that. She worries about working the farm. The two boys are big enough now to be useful. They will cope.

July 23rd – It's a tent city here at Ballarat. Jock and I have decided to build our own hut. Everyone has cut down all the trees around the camp site for firewood and building huts, and also to reinforce all the tunnels they have dug. We will have to go further away to find more wood. You have to be careful walking around the camp at night as the land is full of holes where miners have unsuccessfully searched for gold. I fell in one the other night and found it is now being used as a garbage dump. I had muck in my boots and on my trousers. Jock did laugh until I threw something at him.

August 2nd – Wrote to the wife today. I can't go home empty-handed, not after all this time. It's hard to get clean drinking water. All the once-clear streams have been turned cloudy and filthy by the other miners. I suppose this land was once very beautiful—it isn't now. Some of the miners have sheep and cattle they run on the hills around the camp site and sell the meat to the rest of us. I think I saw a traditional Aboriginal person the other day. Don't see many of them around here anymore. They have moved on, not quite sure where though. I own part of this land now, or at least where my mine is. Why can't I find gold?

October 5th – I'm going home. No gold, only lost hope. I'm sure the wife will be pleased I'm coming home.

TARGETING GENERAL CAPABILITIES: CRITICAL & CREATIVE THINKING AND ETHICAL UNDERSTANDING YEARS 5-6 © PASCAL PRESS ISBN: 978-1-925726-251

Reflecting on thinking & processes

What impact did the miners make on the land around them?

a) They made the streams cloudy and undrinkable.
b) They dug holes all around the camp site.
c) They cleared the land around them of trees.
d) They used the holes to bury garbage.
e) All of the above.

What is Bob's opinion about what happened to the Aboriginal people who inhabited the land?

a) They put sheep and cattle on the land to sell to the miners.
b) They made the streams undrinkable to scare away the miners.
c) They sold the miners part of the land, so they could start looking for gold.
d) They moved away—who knows where?

Write a different ending to Bob's diary. What is an alternative ending?

____

____

What if?

What if you could go back in time to talk to the people whose point of view we have not heard? What if you asked one of Bob's children a question? What would they say? Draw yourself asking a question and write the question in the speech bubble below. Draw the child who answered the question and their response to it.

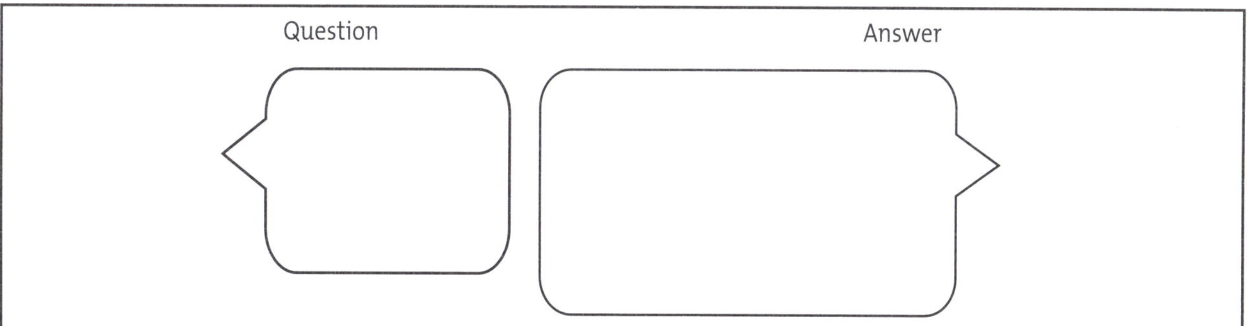

What if you owned a Real Estate Agency and your job was to sell the land around Ballarat in 1852? Draw an advertisement you may have put in the local paper before the goldrush. Then, draw the advertisement you would use to sell the land after the miners had left. How would you sell it?

Ballarat News – Land Sale	Ballarat News – Land Sale

CRITICAL & CREATIVE THINKING

Science – Science as a Human Endeavour

Australian Curriculum Links: *Years 5 & 6 ACSHE083, ACSHE100*

THE OCEAN GAZETTE

The plastic problem

Plastic is a very useful man-made material, but much of our unwanted plastic ends up in the ocean.

Plastic can take 400 years to break down, which makes it a problem that will not go away quickly. There are many different species of animals that are severely threatened because of the amount of plastic waste that ends up in our oceans.

There is even a large collection of plastic and other waste that finds its way into our oceans called the Great Pacific Garbage Patch. It is located in the Pacific Ocean and was discovered in 1997.

This rubbish collects because much of it is not biodegradable. This means it does not decompose or break down naturally. Many plastics do not wear down. They do, however, break down into tinier pieces called microplastics.

The Great Pacific Garbage Patch is nearly impossible to measure as not all of the garbage floats on the surface. Most of the rubbish comes from plastic bags, bottle caps, plastic bottles and Styrofoam cups.

The amount of plastic in the ocean can be very harmful to marine life. Many animals, such as sea turtles, mistake plastic bags for jellyfish, their favourite food. Animals can get entangled in discarded rubbish, such as plastic fishing nets.

Plastic also releases harmful chemicals into the ocean when exposed to prolonged sunlight.

Cleaning up the rubbish in the Great Pacific Garbage Patch would be very expensive and also difficult. Many microplastics are the same size as small sea animals, so nets designed to scoop up the rubbish would scoop them up too.

According to scientists, the best way to clean up the Great Pacific Garbage Patch is to not buy plastic products that can only be used once and to make plastic biodegradable.

What everyone can start doing is: say no to plastic straws, use a reusable water bottle, avoid plastic carry bags and never litter or throw rubbish on the ground.

Credit: iStock-petekarici

1. According to the article, how are we putting marine life in danger?
   a) We are creating plastic waste in our oceans that can be mistaken for food by animals.
   b) We are eating too many fish.
   c) We are using non-biodegradable plastic.
   d) We haven't found the Great Pacific Garbage Patch.
   e) All of the above.
   f) a and c only

2. What does 'biodegradable' mean?
   a) The item stays the same.
   b) The item has to be recycled.
   c) The item has to be plastic.
   d) The item can decompose and break down naturally.

3. What is the Great Pacific Garbage Patch?
   a) It is an island made only from plastic bottles.
   b) It is a large collection of plastic and waste in the Pacific Ocean.
   c) It is a patch of land to bury garbage.
   d) It is something that has been around for a hundred years.

4. List three possible reasons why the Great Pacific Garbage Patch was not discovered until 1997?

____

____

____

CRITICAL & CREATIVE THINKING

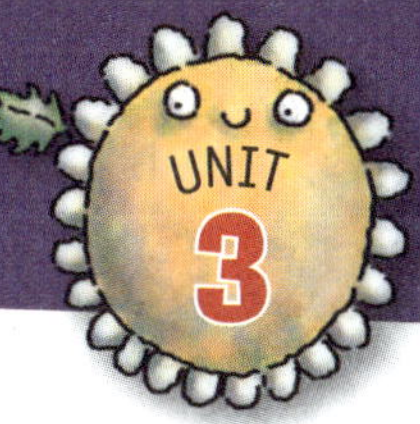

Mathematics – Number and Algebra

Australian Curriculum Links: *Year 5 ACMNA098, ACMNA099 / Year 6 ACMNA123*

Unwanted Plastic

Around 8 million tonnes of unwanted plastic end up in the ocean every year. Another way to represent this is to say 15 garbage trucks full of plastic bottles get emptied into the ocean every minute. How much money is wasted by not recycling the plastic?

1. You and your friends are concerned about the waste of money, and can see a way to help the environment and raise money for a good cause. You want to build a skate park and large playground in the area. Use the table below to calculate the money that you could raise in one day if you took all 15 garbage trucks to recycling. $_______________

2. How much is each bottle worth when recycled? $_______________

3. How many bottles have you collected in 15 garbage trucks? _______________

TRUCKS	BOTTLES	$MONEY
1 truck		
2 trucks		
3 trucks	138,240	
4 trucks		$9216
10 trucks		
15 trucks		

4. As we now know, around 8 million tonnes of unwanted plastic end up in the ocean every year. What does 8 million tonnes look like? How could you represent 8 million tonnes in another way to help others understand how much plastic waste ends up in our oceans?
Write or draw two ways to show 8 million tonnes. For example, you could work out how many elephants or buildings or ...

CRITICAL & CREATIVE THINKING

English – Literacy

Australian Curriculum Links: *Year 5 ACELY1698 / Year 6 ACELY1708*

THE WEEKLY NEWS

DOGNAPPING?

One of Mrs Pug's Afghan Hounds

The gardener of Mrs Hound, Chris Thorn, has been arrested for dognapping the cute and very adorable dog, Henry—pictured just before he disappeared. Henry, a rare and expensive breed, disappeared on Sunday morning, soon after his owner let him out into the backyard of her house in Hedgerow Lane.

Mrs Hound fainted when she discovered that Henry was missing. She has not yet recovered.

A neighbour reported hearing Mrs Hound yell out earlier that morning, 'What are you doing, Chris?' The neighbour, Mrs Pug, who breeds and sells Afghan Hounds and other rare dog breeds to the international community stated, 'I always thought that gardener was a sneaky and untrustworthy person. He's also very rude. He once told me that I was beginning to look just like one of my dogs! Really! I wonder why she hired him! I always wanted to have a gardener, but who can afford one?' she continued.

Mr Thorn denies any involvement in this terrible and nasty act and tried to plead his innocence with his rather feeble statement, I was walking past the property in the morning and did not go inside. Yes, I was in the area, and yes, I stopped at the gate, but why would I take Henry?'

Why indeed?

Henry the dog

The local postwoman, Christine Rettel, who states that she was delivering mail at the time, said, 'I saw him lurking near the open back gate. He was looking suspiciously over his shoulder and seemed to be up to no good. He was moving in a slow and sneaky fashion which shows he was about to commit a crime.'

Mr Christian Hound, the husband of Mrs Hound, had gone for a run that morning and was not on the property at the time.

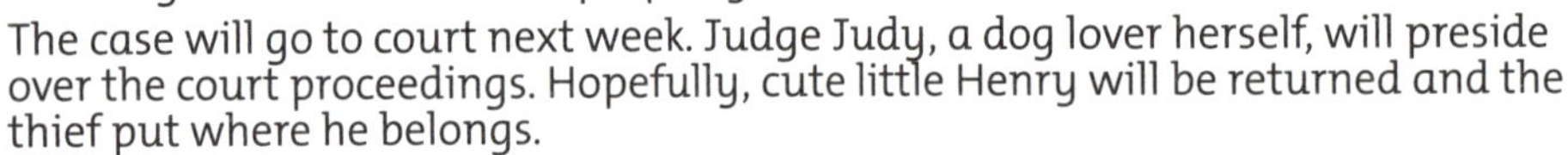

The case will go to court next week. Judge Judy, a dog lover herself, will preside over the court proceedings. Hopefully, cute little Henry will be returned and the thief put where he belongs.

Story by R. E. Porter

Consider your verdict

Read the news article and answer the following questions.

1. The author of this article is trying to persuade people …

   a) to get a gardener.
   b) to buy cute dogs.
   c) that the gardener took Henry.
   d) to buy the paper.

2. Why did the neighbour find Mr Thorn untrustworthy?

   a) She was jealous.
   b) She hated his gardening skills.
   c) He had stopped at the gate.
   d) His eyes were too close together.

3. From the story, why could the judge be a problem for Mr Thorn?

   a) She has TV commitments and won't have time.
   b) She likes dogs and may be biased against Mr Thorn.
   c) She is very cranky and can get angry easily.
   d) She might demand a lot of money.

4. i. Make a list of five words or phrases from the article that try to persuade you.

ii. Now make a list of five words or phrases from the article that are emotional in intent.

5. The paper has put the blame on the gardener. However, from the article, write any reasons why we could be suspicious of the following people:

i. Mrs Pug

ii. The postwoman

iii. Mr Hound

6. Whose voices are not heard and their witness statements are missing?

7. You are the lawyer for Mr Thorn. What questions would you ask the following people to try and prove Mr Thorn's innocence? Write two questions for each.

i. Mrs Pug

ii. Mr Hound

iii. The postwoman

iv. Mr Thorn

Your view

8. Using your device or your notebook, rewrite this article without bias and without emotive language.

9. Who do you think did the crime and why?

Mathematics – Statistics and Probability

Australian Curriculum Links: *Year 5 ACMSP120 / Year 6 ACMSP148*

Identikit: Who took Henry the dog?

A number of witnesses have provided descriptions of a person who was observed opening Mrs Hound's gate and walking away carrying a small dog under their arm.

You can help identify the person who may have snatched Henry, the dog. Match the descriptions given by the five witnesses with the identikit pictures that the Police Artist has drawn. By crosschecking the witness descriptions, you will help the Detectives eliminate anyone not involved in the suspected dognapping. Look for clues or evidence that point to the person who took Henry, the dog.

WITNESS STATEMENTS

Witness 1 – I was sitting on the verandah of my house on the corner of Hedgerow Lane and Trees Street, opposite the park. When all wattle trees are in bloom, I suffer from severe hayfever and have to take medication. My nose is always bright red and running. I notice noses! I know for sure the person I saw crossing the park didn't have a large nose.

Witness 2 – As I was walking to my letterbox to check if the postie had delivered any mail, I saw the back of a person's head as they walked behind a tall hedge in the lane and I am sure they were not wearing a hat.

Witness 3 – I was waiting at the bus stop on the corner of Trees Street and I saw a person with a dog under their arm walking towards the park at the end of Hedgerow Lane. I am pretty sure they had light coloured hair. It wasn't black or brown.

Witness 4 – I was walking in the park and I saw a person hurrying towards the park playground. As they passed near me, I could have sworn I heard a dog bark, but I couldn't see any dogs running around. I know they did not have red hair as I myself have red hair, and I always notice fellow redheads.

Witness 5 – I was surprised to see the postwoman on a Sunday as deliveries are only on weekdays. I called out to my neighbour, Mrs Pug, but there was no answer. I then noticed someone standing near Mrs Hound's gate. I thought I recognised the person but was not sure as I wasn't wearing my glasses. However, I am sure that the person wasn't wearing glasses either.

Witness 6 – I am a hairdresser on Trees Street opposite the park and I could not help but notice a woman crossing the road to the park. She had the most glorious head of hair.

Use the Identikit pictures below and the Elimination Grid on the next page to help you solve this mystery.

Elimination Grid

	gender	red hair	black hair	brown hair	hat	glasses	nose
A							
B							
C							
D							
E							
F							
G							
H							
I							

After using the Elimination Grid, you should have identified the dognapper. Re-read the original news story on page 22 and choose the dognapper from the list below.

a) Chris Thorn, the gardener
b) Christine Rettel, the postwoman
c) Mrs Pug, the neighbour
d) Mr Hound, the husband
e) Mrs Hound, Henry's owner
f) someone unknown

Re-read the description of the dognapping incident and the witness statements. From the information you gather, draw the crime scene showing the streets and where all the witnesses were at the time. Include the dognapper leaving the scene with Henry under their arm. Refer to the answers on page 61 for Scene of the crime, Clothes in the bin activity for an example of how you might draw the scene.

HASS – History

Australian Curriculum Links: *ACHASSK107 / Year 6 ACHASSK135*

STURT'S STORY

Charles Sturt is an explorer of inland Australia. In this expedition he travelled between 1828–1829.

(Based on Volume 1 of Charles Sturt's Two Expeditions into the interior of Southern Australia.)

On returning to camp, we found that the camp was surrounded by native men, looking in wonder at the cattle and horses we had brought with us on the journey of exploration. The native men did not come round the tents but stood in a row at a short distance. At sunset, they gained a little courage and wandered about a little more; at length they went off to the Darling River.

It was quite dark when I heard a native call from the hill, so I sent one of our team, Fred, to find out what the native man wanted. Fred soon returned with a blanket, which he said the native man had returned to him. The native was alone, and when he offered the blanket to Fred, he kept his spear raised in his right hand. However, after seeing that he was not going to be hurt by Fred, he lowered his weapon and walked away.

I was extremely pleased at this trait of honesty shown by the native man, and I was determined to reward it. I found that my men had washed their blankets earlier that day and that one of the blankets had been flung over a bush to dry, hanging over the bank of the river. One of the natives must have pulled it down and took it with him.

In the morning, at about eight, the native men made their appearance on the hill and seemed to be doubtful whether to approach nearer. I went out to them and, with a hand movement, asked them to come closer. I then got them in a row and asked Fred to single out the man who had given him the blanket. After walking two or three times along the line, Fred stopped before one man and put his hand on his shoulder. We then brought out the blanket and explained, with assistance from Mr Hume, that I was highly pleased that they had returned the blanket and presented the native with a small axe and a knife. I wanted to show that I was fair and just and that I rewarded honesty. The other natives were perfectly aware of why I acted like I did, and all of them seemed very pleased that I rewarded the honesty that the man had shown.

Source: adapted from http://gutenberg.net.au/ebooks/e00059.html

Consider your verdict

1. What led to the gift of an axe and a knife?

   a) Sturt did not want any more blankets to be stolen.
   b) Sturt felt sorry for the man who took the blanket.
   c) Sturt wanted to reward honesty and show himself as just and fair.
   d) Sturt wanted to make the Aboriginal people like him.

2. Why were the Aboriginal men pleased to see Sturt present a reward?

   a) It meant that if they stole, they would get a reward.
   b) They thought they would all get a reward.
   c) They liked the man who received the gift.
   d) They were pleased that honesty was rewarded.

3. List five qualities Sturt would need to be an explorer and leader of his men.

____

____

____

____

MY UNCLE'S STORY

My uncle told me a story of the time he met strange ghost-like men by the river. They had brought strange beasts with them that they could control and wore strange layers on their skin. One night, my uncle found one of their skins on a bush and took it. He brought it back to camp and showed some of the other men and the elders. That was when my uncle found himself in trouble—no-one steals in our society, not even from strange creatures that invade our land. The men didn't want these creatures to stay. They wanted them to move out of our land but stealing from another tribe is not right. My uncle then had to show courage and return the skin, not knowing if they would punish him. It turned out that they gave him gifts. The elders knew that the strangers did the right thing, so they let them pass through our land without any further trouble.

4. Why did Uncle have his spear raised when he gave back the blanket?
   a) He was afraid he would be hurt by Fred for taking the blanket.
   b) He wanted to show he was not afraid of Fred.
   c) He wanted to keep the blanket.
   d) He wanted another blanket.

5. Why do you think Uncle called Sturt and his men 'invaders'?

____

____

____

6. Why do you think Uncle called the explorers 'ghost-like men'?

____

____

____

Compare the pair

7. Create a one pager to compare the two stories. Use a blank piece of paper, coloured pencils and pens. Your page must be visually appealing with writing large enough to be easily seen. Include the following on the page:
   i. Draw two sketches to represent the setting. Draw one from the Aboriginal perspective of their land and include one symbol and one word to describe it. Then draw one from Sturt's perspective as an explorer, include one symbol and one word to describe it.
   ii. Using the word 'Same', use pictures and symbols to show what both stories have in common.
   iii. Using the word 'Different', use pictures and symbols to show what is different in both stories.
   iv. In the middle of the page, put a symbol of what you think the stories are about. Label this with one word.

CRITICAL & CREATIVE THINKING

Inquiring, exploring & organising information & ideas – Unit 1

This unit was about, 'Why is it so?' Asking questions is important to find out all the information so that you can seek solutions and solve problems.

Pose questions

1. You are going to interview the characters in the story, Murder, on page 4. Write three questions that you could ask the farmer, the fox and the chicken to get a clearer idea of what went on from each character's point of view.

   i. The farmer ______________________________

   ii. The fox ______________________________

   iii. The chicken ______________________________

2. In the story, To Catch a Thief, on page 5, what do you think would cause the police officer to turn to crime?

   ____

   ____

   ____

   ____

3. Imagine that you are a reporter for the local news channel, and you are interviewing the detective in charge of the investigation. Create questions using the sentence starters below that will help you gather information about the crimes to inform your audience.

   When ______________________________

   Where ______________________________

   What ______________________________

   How ______________________________

   Who ______________________________

   Why ______________________________

TARGETING GENERAL CAPABILITIES: CRITICAL & CREATIVE THINKING AND ETHICAL UNDERSTANDING YEARS 5-6 © PASCAL PRESS ISBN: 978-1-925726-251

Critical & Creative Thinking Assessments

Identify and clarify information and ideas

Conduct a survey to find out where in your state your family would like to holiday for one week. Ask everybody to give their top three ideas.

Family member	Holiday Idea 1	Holiday Idea 2	Holiday Idea 3
1			
2			
3			
4			
Total			

Identify from the survey information the most popular holiday destination and ask your family to help you plan an itinerary that includes:

i. travel time to and from the location
ii. how you will travel there
iii. where you will stay
iv. three activities that you will all do together.

Day 1	Day 2	Day 3	Day 4	Day 5	Day 6	Day 7

Organise and process information

Using your research skills and information from family members, prepare a holiday budget in the table below. Things to consider:

- How many people will be travelling to the holiday?
- What transport will you use to get there and how much will it cost? (car fuel, plane ticket or bus fares)
- Where will you stay? What type of accommodation and how much will it cost? (tent, motel, family cabin)
- What types of activities will interest your family and how much will they cost per person?
- What will you eat and drink on your holiday? Will you be able to cook some meals or will all meals be bought?

Accommodation	Transport	Activities	Food/Meals

ASSESSMENT

Generating ideas, possibilities & actions – Unit 2

This unit asked, 'What if?' and was about imagining possibilities, considering alternatives and seeking solutions.

Imagine possibilities and connect ideas

What if you woke up on a prison ship bound for Australia?

1. Think about how you would feel and what would be going through your mind. Write a diary entry to describe your thoughts and feelings.

2. Re-read John Hudson's story on page 11. Imagine that you were on the same ship as him. What if you had the power to go back in time and change what happened to John Hudson? Write down what you would tell the judge to convince him to release John and not send him as a convict to Australia. You can find more information at: sydneylivingmuseums.com.au/stories/first-fleet-ships/john-hudson.

Consider alternatives

3. What if you were appointed as Governor of a new convict penal settlement in Australia in 1788? You have full authority to plan a new approach of treating convicts. You understand that these people are Australia's first white settlers and that they will need to learn to make their new life in Australia. Research using this site: sydneylivingmuseums.com.au/convict-sydney/day-life-convict to find out how convicts were treated. List three things in the table below that you would do to make life better for the convicts in your care.

Ideas	What would you do?
1	
2	
3	

TARGETING GENERAL CAPABILITIES: CRITICAL & CREATIVE THINKING AND ETHICAL UNDERSTANDING YEARS 5-6 © PASCAL PRESS ISBN: 978-1-925726-251

4 In 2020, people are famous for being sports stars, movie stars, reality TV stars and entertainers. What if you could create a new idea of fame? What sort of people and jobs would you decide are famous? Make a list of your top 5 and give a reason why you think they should be famous.

Your new famous people and jobs	Reasons why
1	
2	
3	
4	
5	

Seek solutions and put ideas into action

5 Look back at your work on page 15, where you drew your face on a bank note. What if money no longer had any value? On the Mind Map below, brainstorm alternatives to money.

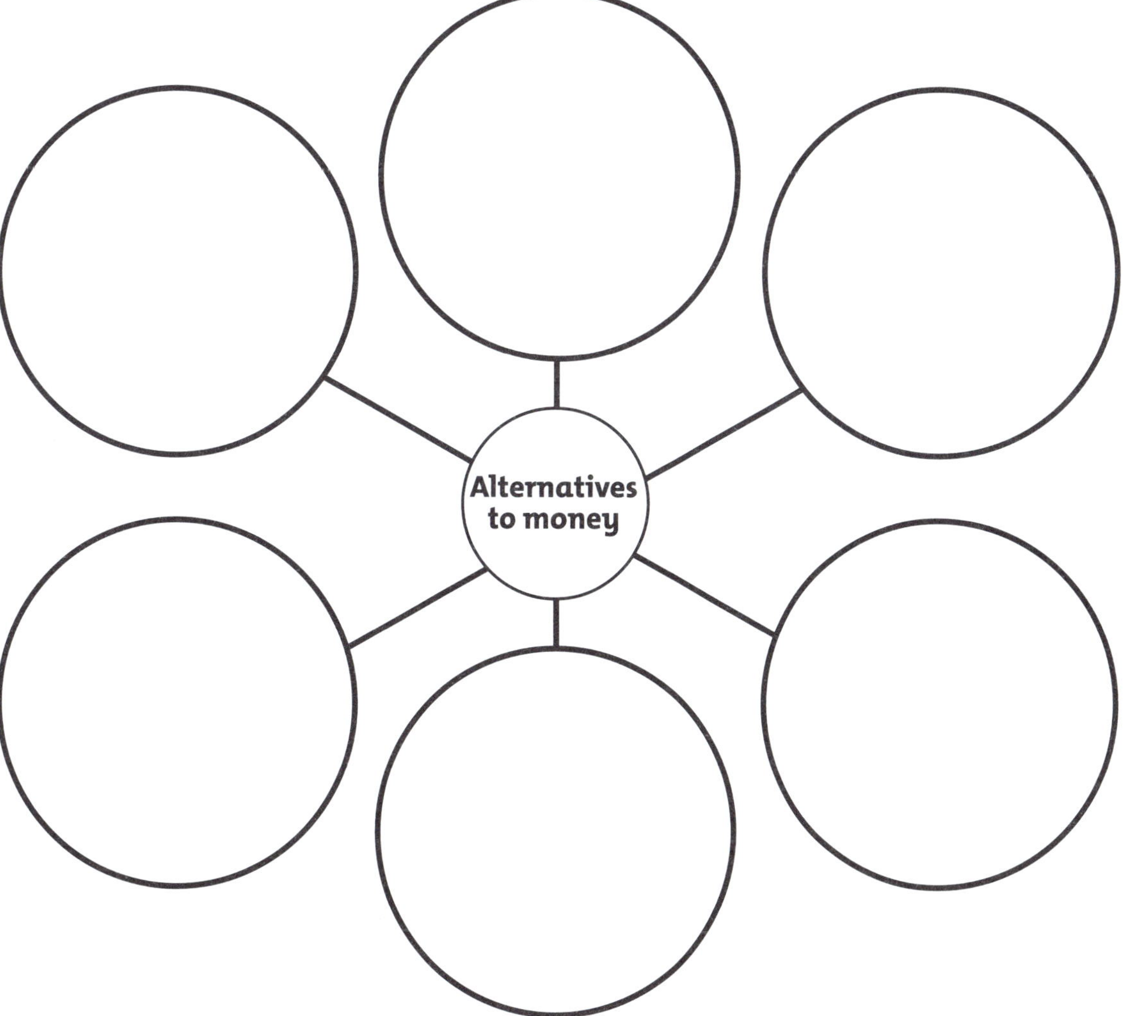

6 Survey your family and friends to see which of your alternative money ideas they think would work the best and why. On the Mind Map, number your ideas in order of popularity and write beside each the reasons they gave for choosing that one.

Reflecting on thinking & processes – Unit 3

This unit was about, 'Thinking about your thinking'. It was about metacognition and reflecting on processes and transferring knowledge into new contexts.

Think about thinking (metacognition)

When you read the story, Chocolate Mines are Running Low, on page 16, you had to think whether the information presented was real or fake news. Fake news is false information that may appear to be true. It can be difficult to determine if something is fake news.

Fake news has been around for centuries, it is not something new. One example is on 21 August 1835, a paper in America, called The New York Sun, published a series of articles about the discovery of life on the moon. The article reported that a well-known astronomer had made the discovery using a new type of telescope. The news article described in great detail the strange life forms inhabiting the moon. These included small reindeer-like animals, horned bears, and beavers walking on two legs. Many people believed the articles and subscribed to the newspaper so that they could keep up with the new discoveries. After a month and after gaining a lot more readers, the paper finally informed the public that it was a hoax.

Source: https://www.thesocialhistorian.com/fake-news/

One of the images that accompanied the news articles

Source: https://www.history.com/this-day-in-history/the-great-moon-hoax

1. Why do you think people in 1835 would believe the newspaper article? Come up with three reasons why.

   i. ______________________________

   ii. ______________________________

   iii. ______________________________

2. Why would people in the 21st century be more likely to not believe this article? Come up with three reasons why.

   i. ______________________________

   ii. ______________________________

   iii. ______________________________

3. The paper wanted to increase the number of people who subscribed to it. Do you think the fake news articles were a good way to do this? Write at least two reasons for and two reasons against the idea using the T bar below.

Why was it a good idea?	Why was it not a good idea?

TARGETING GENERAL CAPABILITIES: CRITICAL & CREATIVE THINKING AND ETHICAL UNDERSTANDING YEARS 5-6 © PASCAL PRESS ISBN: 978-1-925726-251

Reflect on processes

Page 18 outlined some of the problems associated with the goldrush and the environmental impacts goldmining had on the surrounding area. Page 20 showed the Great Pacific Garbage Patch and how our love of plastic has impacted on the environment. Every action we take has a consequence whether positive or negative.

We need to think about what we do and whether the reasons we undertake our action is appropriate. Do the means justify the end? That means, is the result so good or important that it doesn't matter who or what suffered as a consequence of achieving it? This is where you really need to think about your thinking.

In the box below are some examples. Think about each one and decide if the means justify the ends. Include some notes about why you think that.

Means – what you did	Ends – what you wanted	Did the means justify the ends?
After a visit to the vet, you put a plastic cone around your dog's neck. It irritated and annoyed your dog.	It stopped your dog from chewing the stitches that the vet had put in, so the wound healed.	i.
The orthodontist put braces on your teeth for two years. The braces stopped you from eating some of your favourite foods and sometimes made you feel self-conscious.	After two years, your teeth are straight, and you have a stunning smile.	ii.
You ask your parents to create a poster for part of a presentation you have to make because you have run out of time.	You score high marks for your presentation, especially for your poster.	iii.
At a family party, you tell your sister that all the pieces of the birthday cake are equal in size as you pass her a piece of cake.	Not all the pieces are equal in size as you said, so you are able to choose the largest slice.	iv.
You gather up all the clothes and toys left on the floor in your room and shove them in the cupboard in one pile.	You have friends coming over. When they come to your bedroom, they think your room is tidy and that you are a very neat person.	v.
You give your dad the chocolate you dislike most from the box of mixed chocolates.	The chocolates left in the box are your favourites.	vi.

ASSESSMENT

Analysing, synthesising & evaluating reasoning & procedures – Unit 4

In Unit 4 you read about a possible dognapping and were asked to help identify the dognapper by reading the witness statements. You had to analyse the information, consider your verdict and make a decision about who the culprit was.

The two stories set in the past, Sturt's and Uncle's stories, asked you to draw conclusions from the information provided.

Apply logic and reasoning

At times there were clues in the stories that were not relevant and could confuse you. This type of unnecessary information is sometimes called a 'red herring'. It interferes with your ability to think logically and make clear decisions.

1. Use a device to look up the definition of a 'red herring' and write it in your own words.

____

____

____

____

2. Re-read the story, Dognapping?, on page 22. Now that you have worked out that Mrs Pug took Henry, sort out which statements are red herrings and therefore were misleading or distracting and made it difficult for you to come to a conclusion about who did the crime. On the table below, list three red herrings and three useful clues.

Red Herring – not useful information	Useful information
1	
2	
3	

Draw conclusions and design a course of action

Red herrings are often used in stories to send the reader in a different direction. However, in advertising, opinions can be written to sound like facts.

Most people love eating burgers and there is a lot of advertising to make people hungry and want to buy one. Look at the following advertisement.

HEALTH IN A BURGER

- More than a meal
- 100% natural ingredients
- Homemade sauces like Grandma makes
- The best burger in Australia
- All Australian beef
- Meets all your daily nutrition needs
- Your taste buds will love you
- You won't want fries with this one

 Design your own advertisement using the phrases above and the illustration provided. Arrange the statements in a way to make people want to buy the burger.

 Re-read the advertising statements and decide what you think is a fact which could be proved, and what is just an opinion. Use the T bar below to record your answers.

Fact – can be proven	Opinion

Evaluate procedures and outcomes

 On page 24, you had to use an identikit (the pictures) to work out what somebody looked like. Read the text below and fill in the missing words from the word bank.

Word Bank

facial convicted remembering innocent accurately decisions imagine reliable

A study has found that we are better at ______________ faces when we think of the whole face rather than feature by feature. How ______________ do you think the witness statements were, considering the witnesses only saw the people for a few seconds?

Close your eyes for a minute. Think of a person you see all the time and try to ______________ what his or her nose looks like. Think about the shape, size and any particular markings, e.g., a scar. Could you draw their nose ______________?

Now imagine you only have a few seconds to look at a stranger and then you are asked to construct an identikit. You will find it is not that easy, right? Many people have been ______________ because they were wrongly identified using an identikit picture.

To help solve the problem, scientists have created a computer program that has put together lots of different ___________ features to create a collection of different types of faces. The scientists' job is to try to make the identikit as accurate as possible so that ______________ people won't be mistakenly accused of a crime. Scientists know that poor-quality pictures used in identikit photos, affect the ______________ people make when trying to identify a suspect.

By creating a computer program that creates lots of different faces with different facial features, scientists may create more realistic pictures.

Ethical Understanding

Through developing Ethical Understanding Capability, children learn to identify and investigate the nature of ethical concepts, values and character traits, and understand how reasoning can assist ethical judgement. As outlined in the curriculum, the elements and sub-elements are:

 **Understanding ethical concepts and issues** — recognise ethical concepts; explore ethical concepts in context

 **Reasoning in decision-making and actions** — reason and make ethical decisions; consider consequences; reflect on ethical action

 **Exploring values, rights and responsibilities** — examine values; explore rights and responsibilities; consider points of view

TARGETING GENERAL CAPABILITIES: CRITICAL & CREATIVE THINKING AND ETHICAL UNDERSTANDING YEARS 5-6 © PASCAL PRESS ISBN: 978-1-925726-251

Health & Physical Education – Personal, Social and Community Health

Australian Curriculum Links: *Years 5 & 6 ACPPS054, ACPPS055, ACPPS056*

Is lying ever justified?

1

2

3

4

Source: www.ethicsfun.com

Read the cartoon and answer the following questions.

 In frame 1, where does the meeting take place? How do you know? What are the clues?

____

 What clues can you see in frames 1 and 2 that tell you how the girl and father are feeling about the situation?

____

 In frame 2, the girl is thinking, 'I only wanted to please you by getting better grades'. What other strategies could she have used instead of cheating to get better grades and therefore pleasing her father?

____

 In frames 3 and 4, where do you think this takes place? How do you know? What are the clues?

____

 What clues can you see in frames 3 and 4 that tell you how the girl and father are feeling about the situation?

____

 How is the situation different now, compared to frames 1 and 2?

____

 If you were an adult, how would you answer the question the girl asked in frame 4?

____

Health & Physical Education – Personal, Social and Community Health & Movement and Physical Activity

Australian Curriculum Links: *Years 5 & 6 ACPPS056, ACPMP069*

Is lying ever justified?

Now it's your turn. Read each situation below and decide how to respond. Write your responses in the speech bubbles provided.

Situation 1	Situation 2
LOCAL SWIMMING POOL Adults $6 entry. Children under 10 years half price. Hey mum, my 11th birthday was two weeks ago. What should we pay?	If you didn't like the gift, what would be your reply? Didn't you just love what I gave you on your birthday! It was great wasn't it? I wish I had one.
Situation 3	**Situation 4**
You and your friends were playing around in the classroom when one of you accidently knocked over the teacher's plant. When the teacher comes back she is upset and asks who was responsible. Oh no, my pot plant is broken. Does anyone know what happened?	It's the final match in your lunchtime handball game. You're up against the school champion, Talia, whose final serve could win the game. Your class is chanting your name and you are desperate to win. Talia's ball lands just inside the line at the back of the court. However, because you are blocking their view, no-one else can see clearly. Talia asks you if it is in or out. What will you say?

TARGETING GENERAL CAPABILITIES: CRITICAL & CREATIVE THINKING AND ETHICAL UNDERSTANDING YEARS 5-6 © PASCAL PRESS ISBN: 978-1-925726-251

English – Literacy & Science – Science Inquiry Skills

Australian Curriculum Links: *Year 5 ACELY1698, ACELY1699, ACSIS091 / Year 6 ACELY1708, ACELY1709, ACSIS108*

Missions to Mars

THE NEW NEWS

Finding the new and making it news!

WAS THE MOON LANDING A HOAX?

In 1969, NASA sent astronauts to land on the moon but many do not believe this happened.

A group of people believe that NASA faked the landing on the moon by Apollo 11. They believe that NASA could not safely land a man on the moon at that time, as promised by their president. They believe that NASA only sent astronauts into orbit around Earth and sent actors into a movie studio to film the so-called landing.

This theory has been around for over 50 years and still persists today. Those who believe this theory argue that there is evidence on the film footage and photos of the landing which clearly show it was staged and is fake.

One piece of evidence included a mysterious letter C, visible on a moon rock. There were also odd markings on some of the photos given to the media which looked like they had been taken on Earth, not the moon.

Hoax believers ask questions.

Full details of the launch and landing of the LIES mission will be covered by our Science Reporter, Matilda Marsden.

Despite these clues all being disproven, there are people who still persist in believing that the landing was a hoax.

However, the proposed landing of astronauts on Mars by the Australian Government Space Agency (ASA) funded company, Logistical Interplanetary Exploration of Space (LIES), is eagerly awaited.

As we are now in the 21st century, there are no concerns about the company's ability to achieve this successful mission to Mars.

Source: https://the day.co.uk/stories

After reading the article answer the following questions. (Try to answer without researching first and then look up the information to check your answers.)

1. What do the letters NASA stand for? ____________________

2. What was Apollo 11 and what did it do?

   a) Apollo 11 is the name of an astronaut who landed on the moon.

   b) Apollo 11 is the name of the moon mission and rocket used to reach the moon.

   c) Apollo 11 is the name of the launch site.

   d) Apollo 11 is a feature on the moon the astronauts had to explore.

3. After reading the article, decide whether you believe the moon landing was real or a hoax. Explain your reasoning.

   ____

   ____

4. What is the difference between a real event and a hoax?

   ____

   ____

5 Complete the T chart.

Information that supports the landing was a hoax	Information that supports the landing actually happened

6 DID THEY GO OR NOT? WAS THE LAUNCH REAL OR NOT? SHOULD THE REPORTER, MATILDA MARSDEN, REVEAL THE TRUTH?

The New News Reporter, Matilda Marsden needs your help to finish her investigative report on the LIES Mars Mission. Read the following news articles and emails. Matilda has not completed one of her news reports. You need to help her decide whether the mission happened or not so that she can finish her report.

Was the whole thing faked—another hoax? After reading all the reports and emails, finish writing the final part of the news article, 'Is the L.I.E.S. Mars Mission Just Lies?' on page 41. Use the space provided in the article.

Here are some questions to help you plan what to write in the article:

- What would they use the special effects for?
- Did they do the right thing to save people's lives?
- What's wrong with the filtering system?
- Could the emails be fake? Check carefully for clues.
- How did the nation feel about the Mars Mission?

Record your thinking about these questions.

____

____

____

____

THE NEW NEWS

Finding the new and making it news!

AUSTRALIA'S MISSION TO MARS

by Matilda Marsden, Science Reporter

LIES Mars mission puts Australia ahead in the race to Mars.

On 15 October last year, the Australian government funded company, *Logistical Interplanetary Exploration of Space* (LIES), launched their crewed mission to land on and explore the surface of Mars, before returning to Earth.

The mission was expected to take about 21 months—9 months to get there, 3 months on Mars, and then 9 months to get back to Earth.

The world, and especially Australia, has watched the landing and exploration of the surface of Mars with great interest and excitement. It was with great relief that the spacecraft successfully blasted off the Martian surface and the crew is now safely on their way back home.

The LIES rocket on its way to Mars

The New News Science Reporter, Matilda Marsden, will prepare a special report to share with readers after interviewing the LIES crew.

THE NEW NEWS

Finding the new and making it news!

IS THE L.I.E.S. MARS MISSION JUST LIES?

An investigative report by Science Reporter, Matilda Marsden

Leaked emails lead to questions about whether the LIES Mars mission actually happened.

A government 'whistleblower' has released sensitive email conversations between *Logistical Interplanetary Exploration of Space* (LIES) company representative, John Rocket, and T. Orbit from the Australian Space Agency (ASA).

An intensive investigation of the contents of these leaked emails, rather than providing answers, has led to more questions!

Are the emails real or fake? Do these emails provide clear evidence that LIES and ASA were conspiring to replicate the original hoax?

Hoax or fact? Is this just a repeat of the 1969 hoax story?

You be the judge!

Finish the report

____

____

____

____

____

____

____

____

Email 1: 29 February 2019

To: John Rocket – LIES

From: T. Orbit – ASA Director

Subject: MARS Mission Must Succeed

Hi John

Can we meet to plan for success of the LIES Mars Mission?

The engineers have found some leakage within the rocket filtering systems. They don't think the filters will be able to stop microbes and viruses from Mars coming back to Earth. It could be a disaster.

We need a plan because we're too far in, and the eyes of the world are on us.

We have a team from the film unit who know all about special effects. We could make it look real! It could work!

Yours

T. Orbit

Email 2: 1 April 2019

To: T. Orbit – ASA

From: John Rocket – LIES

Hi Tabar

I think the plan is far too risky. We're talking people's lives here! Too many people would have to be involved. The media will be all over it.

We're running out of time too. The launch is scheduled for 15 October.

How could we pull it off in such a short time? I don't like this at all.

John R

Email 3: 31 June 2019

To: John Rocket – LIES

From: T. Orbit – ASA Director

Hello again John

Everything's in place. The film unit have set up an amazing space for the interview. We've managed to get some real spacesuits and moon rocks.

It's all go for October 15! We'll make the nation proud and the media will love it. No-one need ever know.

Tabar Orbit

English – Literacy

Australian Curriculum Links: *Year 5 ACELY1698 / Year 6 ACELY1708*

Real Estate Space Agent – Is lying ever justified?

You are a Real Estate Agent. You have sold all the houses in your areas and after reading about the Mission to Mars, you have a brainwave! Why not be the first Real Estate Space Agent? To get your plan off the ground, you need to think about advertising.

1. Design an advertisement for your new business. You can use the space on this page or make a digital version. Your advertisement should include:
   - **a catchy business name so people know what you do**
   - **a logo that represents your name and your business mission**
   - **a catchy phrase, e.g., Looking for space, try outer space! or Head to Mars. Who needs cars?**
   - **a description of what you are actually selling, e.g., craters, land, Mars rovers etc.**
   - **an idea of the costs and a payment plan.**

My Space Real Estate Advertisement

2. ## Wait a minute!

a) Who owns Mars?____

b) Should anyone be allowed to sell or own parts of Mars? Why? Why not?

____

c) Would you or your family pay money for a piece of Mars? Why? Why not?

____

____

d) Look back at your advertisement. Are advertisements always truthful? What about yours? Is there any part of it that could be considered a lie? Jot down your thoughts below.

____

____

English – Language & The Arts – Media Arts

Australian Curriculum Links: *Year 5 ACELA1502, ACELA1507, ACAMAM062, ACAMAM064 / Year 6 ACELA1518, ACAMAM062, ACAMAM064*

King Solomon

Stories about people in the past may not always be reliable. It is not so simple to say, 'This is what really happened in the past'. Historians know that history tells stories, and these stories are rarely without problems. It's often difficult to piece together different people's versions of the 'truth'. History can be remembered differently by different people or be difficult to recover if no-one is alive to tell their account. At times, it can even be invented.

One such story is the story of King Solomon, a fabulously wealthy and wise king of Israel who lived over 3000 years ago. Stories about him are found in the Bible. Some historians believe he is partly a myth, while others try to piece together evidence to prove his existence. Whether he really existed or not, there is a famous story about how he solved a difficult problem.

One day, while he was sitting in his court, two mothers came to him. Both lived in the same house and both had infant children. One of the children had died in the night, and the two women lay claim to the remaining child. They were brought in front of the king who was asked to solve the problem. The king called for a sword. Solomon declared his judgement: the baby would be cut in two, each woman to receive half. With this strategy, he was able to work out who was not the mother as she entirely approved of this proposal. The actual mother begged that the sword might be put away and the child committed to the care of her rival. The king then gave the baby to the rightful mother.

1. How did King Solomon decide who was the real mother?
   a) The real mother wanted the baby shared.
   b) The real mother would rather give up the baby than have it killed.
   c) The real mother did not want the baby.
   d) The real mother gave King Solomon the sword.

2. The king used the idea of cutting the child in half because ...
   a) that is what they did 3000 years ago.
   b) they did not believe it would kill the child.
   c) the king wanted to show how to share equally.
   d) the real mother would not want that to happen.

Read the cartoon and answer the following questions.

Source: www.ethicsfun.com

ETHICAL UNDERSTANDING

Reasoning in decision-making & actions

 3 Why would the man and child think the cat was lost in frame 1?

____

 4 What do you see in frame 2 to make you think the red-haired girl had a claim to the cat?

____

5 How were the two girls feeling in frame 3 and how do you know?

____

6 Write two reasons why the solution to the problem given in frame 4, is a good idea.
Good idea

i. ____

ii. ____

Compare the pair

 7 The story and the cartoon are alike because ...

a) both solutions ended up with sharing.
b) both problems dealt with something that had been found.
c) both problems dealt with ownership.
d) everybody was a winner.

 8 The story and the cartoon are different because ...

a) one was deciding who was lying, and the other was how to share.
b) they were in different times in history.
c) not all wanted the best for the child, but all wanted the best for the cat.
d) all of the above.

KING SOLOMON – THE WISE OR THE UNWISE?

 9 Newsfront, a local news program, wants you to interview people about King Solomon. Was he wise or unwise? What if someone carried out his order? Would he then still be considered wise?

Select three people to interview and film the interviews. Write down two questions you will ask each person. Film their responses for the Newsfront program.

Questions you will ask in your interview:

1. ____
2. ____

Health & Physical Education – Personal, Social and Community Health

Australian Curriculum Links: *Years 5 & 6 ACPPS053, ACPPS054, ACPPS055, ACPPS056*

The Gamers

You had just arrived back home after a day at school when you decided to log into the blog that you share with members of your class. When you logged on you saw you had a message from Jo. The message, however, really concerned you and you tried to give Jo some advice. Because you were concerned about his safety, you decided to take a screenshot of it. Read the conversation below.

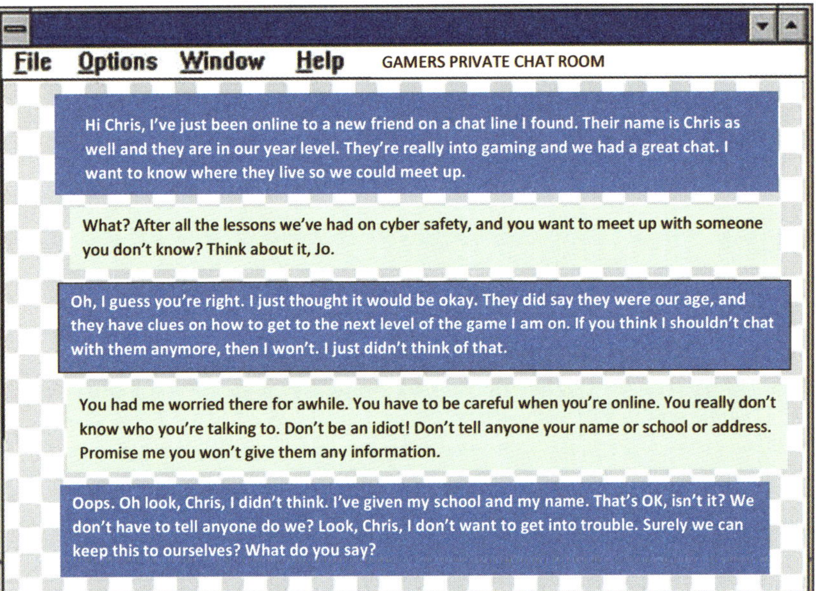

After reading the blog, answer the questions below.

 1 Why is Chris concerned about Jo giving out any personal information?

a) You do not know who is on the other end of the conversation.
b) You may give out information where a person can find you.
c) You need to keep personal information private and share only with friends or trusted adults.
d) You may be putting yourself in danger.
e) All of the above

 2 What advice would you give Jo?

a) Don't worry and do nothing.
b) Try and meet the person you are gaming with to check them out.
c) Get Chris to take his place when gaming with that person.
d) Tell a trusted adult about what happened.
e) Write back to the person online and find out who they are.

3 Write three rules that you think all children should know before they join online blogs or chatrooms.

i. ______________________________
ii. ______________________________
iii. ______________________________

ETHICAL UNDERSTANDING

4 If you were Jo and someone asked you for your name or address, how would you respond? Write down the response you would send.

Later that night, Jo once again messaged Chris with an update on what had happened.

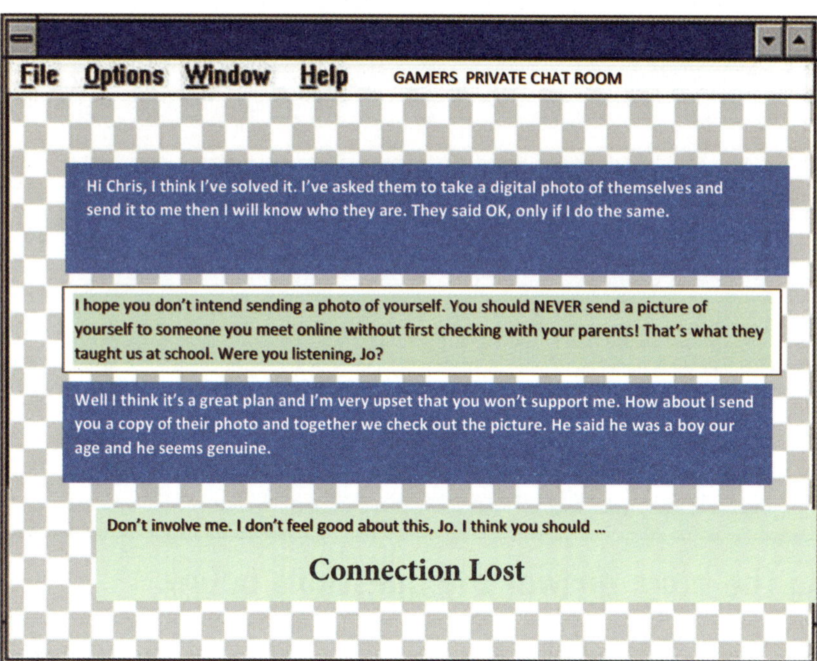

5 Why should you never post a photo of yourself to people you meet online? Write your answer in the box below.

6 Write a positive ending to the conversation. How could they have resolved the situation?

7 List three trusted adults you could talk to if this situation had happened to you.

i. ____________________

ii. ____________________

iii. ____________________

TARGETING GENERAL CAPABILITIES: CRITICAL & CREATIVE THINKING AND ETHICAL UNDERSTANDING YEARS 5-6 © PASCAL PRESS ISBN: 978-1-925726-251

Mathematics – Number and Algebra

Australian Curriculum Links: *Year 5 ACMNA100, ACMNA121 / Year 6 ACMNA123*

CODED MESSAGE

When you open up your games' chatroom, you notice a message for you. When you open it, it just looks like a lot of random numbers until you notice that it could be a coded message. You can see a grid and what looks like spaces for an answer.

To find out what is going on, you have to decode the message by using the clues provided in the grid. After you have worked out the answer for each of the letters of the alphabet record them in the a-z table below.

A = Fill in the missing factor of 24: 1, 24, 8, 4, ?, 6, 2, 12	**B** = $\frac{3}{7} + \frac{4}{7} = \frac{7}{?}$	**C** = Fill in the equivalent fraction: $\frac{5}{20} = \frac{1}{?}$	**D** = $\frac{20}{20}$ = ?
E = What digit is in the 'hundredth' place? 12.456	**F** = $\frac{1}{3}$ of 24 = ?	**G** = Write the equivalent fraction. $\frac{45}{3} = \frac{?}{1}$	**H** = Round this decimal to the nearest whole number: 5.56 =
I = Find the pattern to fill in the missing decimal number: 9.4, 9.6, 9.8, ?	**J** = The area of a rectangle is 24 cm^2. If one side is 2 cm, what is the other side?	**K** = 6 x (4 + 2) – 1 = ?	**L** = $\frac{5}{8} - \frac{1}{8} = \frac{1}{?}$
M = Find the perimeter of a square if one side is 13 cm.	**N** = In digital time, 10:45 is the same as a quarter to ? in analogue time.	**O** = John collected 3 times as many eggs as Susan. Susan had a dozen eggs. How many eggs does John have?	**P** = If there are 360 degrees in a circle, how many degrees are in a quarter of a circle?
Q = 5^2 + (2 x 12.5) = ?	**R** = ? Can you work it out from the words in the message?	**S** = ? Can you work it out from the words in the message?	**T** = ? Can you work it out from the words in the message?
U = $\frac{2}{3} + \frac{5}{12}$ = ? Write your answer as a mixed number.	**V** = Jack owns 84 sets of football cards. Each set has exactly 5 cards. Jack keeps 2/3 of the cards. How many cards does he keep?	**W** = How many degrees in this angle? ?	**X** = $\frac{3}{5}$ of the staff are male. There are 50 staff members. How many of the staff are female?
Y = Round up to the nearest metre. 1629cm = ?	**Z** = Jaxon will be 12 next birthday. He is four years younger than Madoc who is two years older than Aisha. How old is Aisha?		

a	b	c	d	e	f	g	h	i	j	k	l	m	n	o	p	q	r	s	t	u	v	w	x	y	z

Now you have worked out the value for each letter, fill in the spaces below each of the numbers to reveal the full message.

1,5,2,5,9,5 9,6,10,14 52,5,14,14,3,15,5 3,8,9,5,0 0,5,3,1,10,11,15

_ _.

10,9,14 36,11

_ _'_ _ _!!!!!!!!!!

52,5,5,9 3,9 9,6,5 1,0,10,11,35,10,11,15 9,3,90,14 3,8,9,5,0 3,14,14,5,52,7,2,16

_ _

ETHICAL UNDERSTANDING

52,36,12,36 6,3,14 180,3,9,5,0 7,3,2,2,36,36,11,14 5,3,4,6
4

_ _ _ _   _ _ _   _ _ _ _ _   _ _ _ _ _ _ _ _   _ _ _ _

8,10,2,2 9,6,5 7,3,2,2,36,36,11,14 3,11,1, 6,5,3,1 9,36 9,6,5 2,10,7,0,3,0,16 9,36,90

_ _ _ _   _ _ _   _ _ _ _ _ _ _ _   _ _ _   _ _ _ _   _ _   _ _ _   _ _ _ _ _ _ _   _ _ _

8,2,36,36,0 11,5,3,0 9,6,5 36,90,5,11 180,3,2,35,180,3,16

_ _ _ _ _   _ _ _ _   _ _ _   _ _ _ _   _ _ _ _ _ _ _

180,3,10,9 8,36,0 9,6,5 7,5,2,2

_ _ _ _   _ _ _   _ _ _   _ _ _ _

180,6,5,11 9,6,5 35,10,1,14 4,36,52,5 36,1,1/12, 9 3,9,9,3,4,35

_ _ _ _   _ _ _   _ _ _ _   _ _ _ _   _ _ _ _   _ _ _ _ _ _

9,6,5,11 4,2,5,3,0 36,$1\frac{1}{12}$,9 10,9 180,10,2,2 7,5 14,36 8,$1\frac{1}{12}$,11

_ _ _ _   _ _ _ _ _   _ _ _.   _ _   _ _ _ _   _ _   _ _   _ _ _

4,6,0,10,14,90,10,5

_ _ _ _ _ _ _ _

When you are sure you have decoded the message correctly, answer the following questions.

 What is Chrispie's plan?

____

____

3. Sometimes things that sound like fun can end up causing problems and even getting people hurt. Think about the consequences of joining in the plan and use the table below to list three points for and against joining in with the water-bombing plan.

Points for	Points against
• It's fun to do things with your friends. • • •	• Water balloons are hard to fill. • • •

4. Use the same code to write back to Chrispie. Say whether you will join the plan and why.

TARGETING GENERAL CAPABILITIES: CRITICAL & CREATIVE THINKING AND ETHICAL UNDERSTANDING YEARS 5-6 © PASCAL PRESS ISBN: 978-1-925726-251

English – Language and Literature

Australian Curriculum Links: *Year 5 ACELA1512, ACELT1609 / Year 6 ACELA1525, ACELT1613*

The Lunch Box

Read the cartoon and do activities 1–5.

 Write the answer to each question in the box.

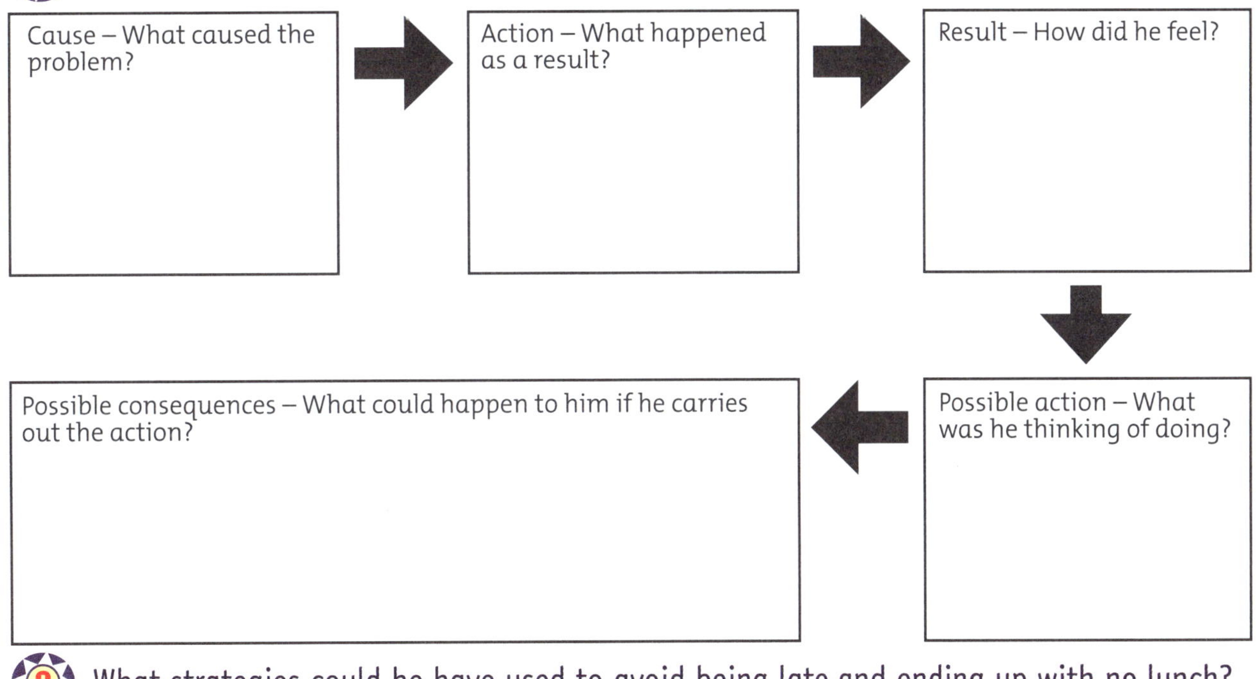

 What strategies could he have used to avoid being late and ending up with no lunch? List three strategies that you use in the morning to avoid being late for school.

1	2	3

ETHICAL UNDERSTANDING

Exploring values, rights & responsibilities

3. The thoughts in your head don't have an effect on anyone if you don't act on them. Re-read the cartoon and think what would happen if the character's thoughts (shown in the speech bubbles) were spoken out loud to the other characters in the cartoon. Choose one or more options below.
   a) His parents would pack him extra food, so he would not miss breakfast.
   b) His parents would drive him to school, so he wasn't late.
   c) His friends would share their lunch.
   d) Kookie would be upset and angry that he stole the lunch.
   e) All of the above

4. Rewrite the cartoon turning his thoughts into speech. How would the other characters respond to him? Fill in their speech bubbles.

Source: www.ethicsfun.com

5. Have you ever been late for school? Were you lost in the fog? Fell asleep in the shower? The dog ate your alarm clock? Write a humorous letter to the teacher explaining why you are late.

Dear Teacher,
I am sorry I am late, but I have a wonderful excuse. It really wasn't my fault.

____

____

____

____

TARGETING GENERAL CAPABILITIES: CRITICAL & CREATIVE THINKING AND ETHICAL UNDERSTANDING YEARS 5-6 © PASCAL PRESS ISBN: 978-1-925726-251

HASS – Civics and Citizenship

Australian Curriculum Links: *Year 5 ACHASSK115 / Year 6 ACHASSK147, ACHASSK148*

Rights of the Child

Thirty years ago, world leaders made an historic commitment to the world's children by adopting the Convention on the Rights of the Child. It has helped transform children's lives around the world. It inspired governments of many countries to change laws and policies and budget for child health care, nutrition and education, and make them safe in society.

In Australia, you have many rights, but you also have responsibilities that go with them. See the table below for some examples. Complete the responsibilities for the last three Rights by writing in the table.

Right	Responsibility
(Article 19) If children have the right to be protected from being hurt or mistreated in body or mind …	then children also have the responsibility not to bully or harm each other.
(Article 24) If children have the right to a clean environment …	then children also have the responsibility to do what they can to look after their environment.
(Article 28) If children have the right to be educated …	
(Article 13) If children have the right to get and share information …	
(Article 24) If children have the right to good quality health care, clean water, nutritious food, and a clean environment to stay heathy …	

In your life, what are your rights and responsibilities? Fill in the table below. The first one has been done for you.

Right	Responsibility
If you have been given the right to drive a car …	then you also have the responsibility to follow the road rules.
If you have been given the right to use a device in the classroom …	
If you have been given the right to join a sporting team …	
If you have been given the right to have a sleepover at a friend's house …	

ETHICAL UNDERSTANDING

Health & Physical Education – Personal, Social and Community Health

Australian Curriculum Links: *Years 5 & 6 ACPPS055, ACPPS056*

KIDS WATCH

Stealing, is it ever right?

Have you ever played a game of 'cops and robbers'? Cops and robbers is a fun, make-believe game, where one person steals something and is chased by others. So, how do we know when stealing is wrong?

Have you or anyone in your family or friends had something stolen? How does this make people feel?

Stealing is when a person takes something that belongs to somebody else without asking permission. We might know the person, or it could be a stranger.

Big or small things can be stolen—a packet of lollies from a shop, a ball from school or lunch from a friend's lunch box.

Most school-aged children know that they aren't supposed to take something without asking or without paying for it. However, some children haven't learnt or may not think of the consequences. They don't even think of asking first before taking something that belongs to someone else.

Some children steal because their friends or family members do it or because they have been dared. They might believe their friends will like them more if they steal.

Sometimes your friends pressure you to do something that you know is not right. Doing something for these reasons is called peer pressure, but you don't have to give in to it.

Talk with an adult—parent, teacher, older brother or sister—about what strategies you could use to help you make the right choices.

Reporter – I M Goodly

ETHICAL UNDERSTANDING

Read the Kids Watch article and complete activities 1 and 2 below.

1 Doing the DAB

The bell goes and you and your friends burst out of the classroom. The new kid is getting their lunch box out of their bag when one of your friends grabs the lunch box and starts handing out the contents to the rest of the group. You are handed a chocolate frog from the lunch box and are told to eat it.

WHAT WILL YOU DO?

Use the DAB strategy to decide what to do.

DEFINE THE PROBLEM	
What is happening?	
How are you feeling?	
How is the owner of the lunch box feeling?	

TARGETING GENERAL CAPABILITIES: CRITICAL & CREATIVE THINKING AND ETHICAL UNDERSTANDING YEARS 5-6 © PASCAL PRESS ISBN: 978-1-925726-251

All the possibilities

List three possible solutions and think what the consequences for each solution might be. How do you think people will feel?

Possible solution	Consequences for this action	Possible feeling people may have after this action
1		
2		
3		

Bound into action

What is your best solution?	Why did you choose this solution?

2 Who stole the cookies?

You and your friends are in the school canteen line. When the adult serving tuns away to serve someone else, the person in front of you reaches into the container on the counter, takes two large cookies and hides them in their pocket. Next, the adult turns back to serve you and notices the cookies are missing and stares at you. The adult says to you, 'There are two cookies missing. Did you take them?' What are you going to do?

Below is a list of possible actions you might take. Circle all the actions you think would be the right thing/s to do.

a) Tell them it was not you.
b) Tell them who stole the cookies.
c) Look confused and ignore what the adult is saying.
d) Look at the other child and wait for them to reply.
e) Run away.
f) Be embarrassed and not know what to say.
g) Deny any knowledge and then make the other person give you a cookie.
h) Deny any knowledge and tell that person's teacher afterwards.
i) Smile slyly and point to the person who stole the cookies.
j) Your own suggestion______________________________.

Technologies – Design and Technologies

Australian Curriculum Links: *Years 5 & 6 ACTDEK019, ACTDEP028*

MISSION POSSIBLE

You are a child genius working for the company, *Lunch Boxes R Us*. Recent research has revealed that kids all around Australia are having problems with their lunch boxes, e.g., lunches are stolen, items fall out and lunches get hot and yucky. It's your job to design a user-friendly lunch box that:

- is as environmentally friendly as possible
- can only be opened by the owner
- will keep lunches fresh in all sorts of weather
- will stop items falling out
- is easy to use
- looks good.

Your task is to:

- think of all the different options technology provides for you to undertake this task
- make a list of three possibilities, e.g., Siri opens your lunch box, password protected and so on.

i. ______________________________

ii. ______________________________

iii. ______________________________

Choose one or more of the possibilities you listed and create a Design Brief that includes:

- reason for the design—the problem that the design will solve
- the technology that you will use
- sketch or plan of your proposal.

DESIGN BRIEF

NAME OF YOUR LUNCH BOX DESIGN ______________________________

SPECIAL FEATURES OF YOUR LUNCH BOX ______________________________

____

THE TECHNOLOGY USED ______________________________

____

SKETCH/PLAN

Understanding ethical concepts & issues – Unit 5

This unit questioned, 'Is lying ever justified?' The stories on pages 37 and 39 looked at the concept of truth and lie. There have been many books and TV programs about lying and telling the truth. However, there is an agreement that lying is a form of deception where the liar:

- communicates some true or false information
- intends to mislead or deceive
- believes that what they are 'saying' is not true.

Recognise ethical concepts

Adults tell children that it is wrong to lie but sometimes they tell a lie (little one or a big one) themselves! This can make it very confusing for children.

1. Describe a situation where you have told a little lie and explain why you didn't tell the truth.

   ____

   ____

2. Think of a time that you know an adult has told a lie or stretched the truth. What was the lie and why do you think it was told?

   ____

   ____

3. People say that a liar needs to have a good memory. What do you think that comment means?

   ____

   ____

4. If lying is giving some information which you know to be untrue, then you are intending to deceive someone by telling a lie. Describe a time when you think it may be OK to tell a lie.

   ____

   ____

5. What harm do lies cause? Read the statements and choose the ones that you think are true. For some of these statements, it will be difficult for you to decide, so discuss them with a family member.

	Statement	True	False	Undecided
a	The person who is lied to will feel deceived and manipulated.			
b	Lies hurt the person who is lied to.			
c	Lies are a necessary part of life.			
d	Everyone lies.			
e	It is OK to tell little white lies to protect someone.			
f	You can always tell when someone is lying.			
g	The information in a lie could actually be true.			

ASSESSMENT

Explore ethical concepts in context

Re-read the article, *Is the L.I.E.S Mars Mission just lies?*, on page 41, and the emails released by a government whistleblower. In Email 1, Tabor Orbit (the ASA director), advises John Rocket (from LIES) that there is some leakage in the rocket filtering system, which could result in microbes and viruses getting back to Earth. You had to think through all the evidence given and work out whether the Australian Mars Mission was a hoax or not. A hoax is a deliberate lie designed to appear truthful.

Social media has lots of examples where people can be tricked into doing something that might end up making them feel embarrassed or looking silly. You think it may be fun to play a hoax challenge on your friend in your class. You make up a fake challenge called 'Frozen by the bell!' where a person, upon hearing the school bell, stands frozen wherever they are in the school. They stay frozen for five seconds and then continues on as normal, as if nothing had happened. You tell your friend that this is the latest craze, and you would film them whenever they do it and post it to social media.

Source: https://www.cultofpedagogy.com/one-pagers/

In the space below, or digitally, create a 'One Pager'. You use colour, images and words to create your vision of what could be the best and worst outcomes of your hoax for your friend and you.

The best consequences that could happen.

HOAX – Describe the hoax using pictures and words.

The worst consequences that could happen.

Reasoning in decision-making & actions – Unit 6

This unit was about, 'What should I do?' It was about making decisions and thinking about the consequences of those decisions or actions that you undertake.

Reason and make ethical decisions

Page 43 was about a very wise king named King Solomon whose decision helped to work out which of the two women was the real mother of the baby brought before him. There are times in our lives where we have to make some hard decisions and it can be difficult working out what the best decision is.

1. Read the following story and think about what you could do in that situation.

Your friend has invited you over for a fun afternoon where you know you will have a good time together. You have your parents' permission to go; however, the only requirement is that you have to get your homework done first. Unfortunately, you have a work assignment to finish. It isn't hard, but it is one of those tasks that will take time if you want to do it well. You could just tell your parents you did the work even though you didn't. They'll never know. Or, you could stay home and finish the assignment but miss out on the fun time with your friend. What will you do? Explain your choice.

____

____

____

2. From the story, there are several phrases to do with making decisions that are used in conversations today. Insert the missing words or phrases that have come from the story of King Solomon into the following text. The words and phrases are listed below. There are more words than spaces in the story.

Word bank

king | judgement of Solomon | getting what you want | split the baby
won the battle | sword of power | Solomon | you can't split the baby
cutting the baby in half | use the sword | superpower of wisdom | wisdom of Solomon

A very wise person can be called a _______________ and can be said to have the _______________ or the _______________. A wise person may need to make a compromise and negotiate with people to get a decision. In a court room, they may call this type of negotiating, _______________. In a courtroom, to say that a wise compromise was made in a difficult disagreement, it can be said to _______________. Could you possibly use this phrase when you are trying to negotiate a good compromise with your family or friends? However, there are times when you cannot come to a compromise, it may be impossible. In this case you would say, '_______________'.

Ethical Understanding Assessments

ASSESSMENT

Consider consequences

Page 45 was about The Gamers who had to think about the consequences of their actions while they were online. Sometimes an adult can see the consequences when you do not. Read the cartoon on the right.

Source: www.ethicsfun.com

 3. Why would the girl's mother have a rule about meeting the parents first? Think of two reasons why she made this rule.

i. ______________________________

ii. ______________________________

 4. Why would Julia's parents let her go? Think of two reasons why.

i. ______________________________

ii. ______________________________

 5. What would be the consequences if there were no rules set by parents or adults? Think of two consequences.

i. ______________________________

ii. ______________________________

Reflect on ethical action

 6. What are the family rules in your house and why has your family made these rules? Name four.

Rule	Reason for the rule
1	
2	
3	
4	

Page 47 had a code for you to decipher and work out the message that was sent to the gang members, by Chrispie. The gang had a plan that may not have been a good choice to be part of. You had to make that decision on page 48. Codes have been used over the years to pass along messages to specific people. Only those who know the code can work out the message. Can you create your own code?

 7. Invent a new code and share it with your family or friends. Ask them to write a message back to you using your code. For example, ?Siht daer uoy nac = Can you read this? You can use this idea or use maths sums or a combination of the two. A grid is provided if you want to use it to help you devise your code.

a	b	c	d	e	f	g	h	i	j	k	l	m	n	o	p	q	r	s	t	u	v	w	x	y	z

Exploring values, rights & responsibilities – Unit 7

This unit was about acting responsibly and thinking about values. It explored the rights of children and our responsibilities.

Examine values and consider points of view

Values are your beliefs which influence your attitude towards things and the way you act. When you have to work out the right action to take, you need to think through all the possible things you could do and what the consequences could be for each. After you have thought about the consequences for each action, you can make a more informed decision. That is what you did on pages 49 and 50 when you read the story of the Lunch Box and on pages 52 and 53 when you used the DAB strategy to help you decide a course of action.

Read the story below and use the DAB strategy to help you decide what to do.

Your class is going on school camp for three days and you are very excited. The night before the camp, you discover small sores on your arm. Your sister had chickenpox last year and these sores look like the ones she had. You also know that some children in another class at school were sent home last week with chickenpox. What do you do? If you tell your parents, you may not be able to go on camp. If you don't tell your parents, there may be other consequences.

Fill in the table below listing possible consequences for each action.

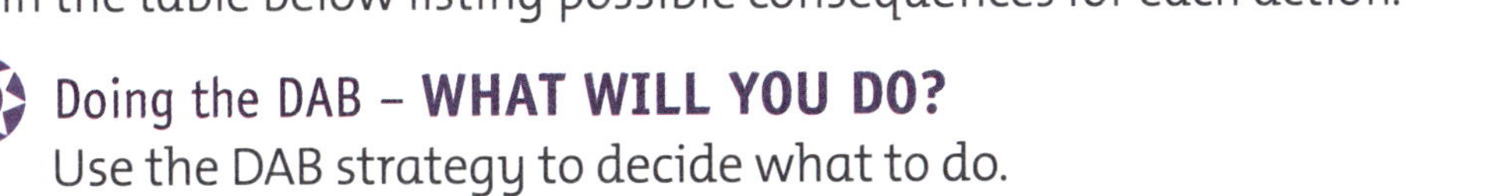

1 Doing the DAB – **WHAT WILL YOU DO?**

Use the DAB strategy to decide what to do.

DEFINE THE PROBLEM	
What is happening?	
How are you feeling?	

ALL THE POSSIBILITIES		
List three possible solutions and think what the consequences for each solution might be. How do you think people will feel?		
Possible solution	Consequences for this action	Possible feeling people may have after this action
1 You show your arm to your parents.		
2 You do not say anything to your parents.		
3 Another solution you can think of		

BOUND INTO ACTION	
What is your best solution?	Why did you choose this solution?

ASSESSMENT

ASSESSMENT

Explore rights and responsibilities

On page 51 in Unit 7, the activities asked you to explore the rights of a child. In this assessment, you will continue to think about the rights you have within your home.

For this activity, you need to think of all the things you would have in an ideal bedroom. You need to picture your ideal bedroom in your mind.

The things you thought of can be put into different categories or groups. These categories are:

- a 'want', which is something that is nice to have; however, it is not necessary or essential
- a 'need', which is something that is necessary to have
- a 'right', which is something that is so important to have that you have a right to expect to have it.

Some of the things you thought of for your ideal bedroom can fall into more than one category. Some things may be a 'want', a 'need' and a 'right', but it is important to know that not all things will be rights.

With every right comes a responsibility that goes with it.

Think of your picture of an ideal bedroom. On the table below, list your ideas under the headings of: wants, needs, and rights. If you listed a 'right", try to write a responsibility that goes with it. Two examples have been included in the table to help you.

Wants	Needs	Rights	Responsibilities
room service			
		clean bedding	Take the dirty sheets to the laundry and make the bed with clean sheets.

Ask an older person what rights they believe are important in the family home. You also need to think about who would be responsible for making sure these rights are respected. From your discussion, fill in the table below.

Family rights	Who is responsible to see the rights are respected?

TARGETING GENERAL CAPABILITIES: CRITICAL & CREATIVE THINKING AND ETHICAL UNDERSTANDING YEARS 5-6 © PASCAL PRESS ISBN: 978-1-925726-251

CRITICAL & CREATIVE THINKING CAPABILITY

Unit 1

Pages 4-5: English – Literacy & Literature

1 c

2 teeth

3 Responses may include: weapon in mouth, sack used as a pillow, more than one wife, family safe underground.

4 b

5 a

6 The detective had already committed the crime and so knew what the scene looked like.

7 They had stolen the bracelet from the jewellery shop and the stone was a diamond.

8 The phone would ring to report another break in as the detective had just come in late after robbing another store.

9 Personal responses will vary.

Pages 6-7: Mathematics – Measurement & Geometry

1 Personal responses will vary.

2 i. giraffe 4.5 m, elephant 2.5 m, rhino 1.5 m, hippo 1.25 m, lion 1 m, YOU __ ii. Personal responses will vary.

3 Personal responses will vary.

Pages 8-9: Science – Science as a Human Endeavour

1 Responses will vary. Below is one example.

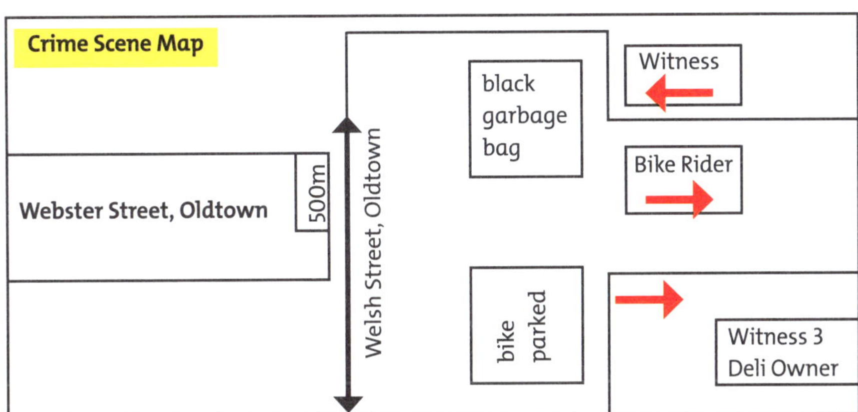

2 Responses will vary but might include: Evidence Tag Item #B333 – Description: Men's polo shirt, light blue with dark blue collar and sleeves, and a three-button opening at the neck. Brand: Lacoste. Location: Found in open black garbage bag in rubbish bin on cnr of Webster & Welsh Streets, Oldtown. Evidence Tag Item #C334 – Description: Men's light blue denim jeans, zip-up. Markings: Tear in back pocket. Location: Found in open black garbage bag in rubbish bin on cnr of Webster & Welsh Streets, Oldtown.

3 Analysis, clothing, jacket, chocolate, microscopic, male, receipt, Repairs, interviewed, alibi, inquiries

4 Responses will vary; however, from the statement given by Witness 3, who either owns or works in the Welsh Street Deli, it is clear that a person in a bike helmet robbed the money from the Deli's cash register and rode off on a bike parked outside. There is not enough evidence to decide if this was the same bike rider who dumped the black garbage bag of clothes in the gutter in Webster Street. There may have been two different bike riders with two different black garbage bags! Mr Robinhood did not have an alibi at the time of the robbery, and although he did have evidence to owning a bike, there is not enough evidence to convict him.

Unit 2

Pages 10-11: HASS – History

1 July 1938

2 b

3 Responses will vary but may include asking: Did you ever have a family in Australia?/What jobs did you work at in Australia?/Did you ever regret coming to Australia?/If you had your time over again, would you have lit the haystack?

4 a

5 c

6 Personal responses will vary.

7 Responses may include: He was scared./He was illiterate and didn't know what to say./He was guilty of the crime./He was only a child.

8 a

9 Personal responses will vary.

Page 12: English – Literacy

1–2 Responses will vary

TARGETING GENERAL CAPABILITIES: CRITICAL & CREATIVE THINKING AND ETHICAL UNDERSTANDING YEARS 5-6 © PASCAL PRESS ISBN: 978-1-925726-251

Page 13: HASS – History

1 Fred Hollows (G)

2 Andy Thomas (H)

3 Kathy Freeman (F)

4 Professor Graeme Clark (A)

5 Dr Fiona Wood (B)

6 Kurt Fearnley (D)

7 Edith Cowan (C)

8 David Unaipon (E)

Page 14: English – Literacy

1–6 Personal responses will vary.

Page 15: The Arts – Visual & Media Arts

1–3 Responses will vary.

Unit 3

Pages 16-17: English – Language

1 d

2 d

3 Personal responses will vary.

Page 19: HASS – History & Geography

1 e

2 d

3–5 Personal responses will vary.

Page 20: Science – Science as a Human Endeavour

1 f

2 d

3 b

4 Responses may include: The Great Pacific Garbage Patch is in an area of the ocean not used by ships./It is not picked up by satellite images./It is not one solid mass./ Most of the garbage is underwater./It may have been found earlier, but it was not publicised.

Page 21: Mathematics – Number and Algebra

1 $34,560

2 5 cents each

3 691,200

4 Responses will vary.

Unit 4

Pages 22-23: English – Literacy

1 c

2 a

3 b

4 i. Words to persuade can include: dognapping, sneaky and untrustworthy, rude, wonder why she hired him, tries to plead his innocence, rather feeble statement, lurking, looking suspiciously, up to no good, slow and sneaky fashion, shows he was about to commit a crime. ii. Words emotional in intent can include: cute and very adorable, rare and expensive, not yet recovered, terrible and nasty act, a dog lover, cute little Henry. Some words can appear in both lists.

5 i. Mrs Pug breeds and sells rare dogs and Henry is a rare dog. Mrs Pug also wants to hire a gardener; however, she doesn't have enough money to do so. Selling Henry could be one way to raise enough money to hire a gardener. ii. The postwoman's name is Christine and the neighbour heard Mrs Hound call out the name, Chris. She said she was delivering mail on a Sunday which is very unusual and was by the back gate of the Hound property as she said she saw Mr Thorn at the gate. iii. Mr Hound had gone for a run in the morning which was the same time the dog disappeared. His name is Christian, and Mrs Hound may have been calling to him when she shouted the name, Chris.

6 The voices not heard are Mr and Mrs Hound.

7 Responses will vary and may include the following:

Mrs Pug – Who do you think Mrs Hound meant when she called out the name, Chris? Are you jealous of the Hounds having a gardener and is that why you dislike Mr Thorn? Did you take Henry to sell to the international market?

Mr Hound – Was Henry in the yard when you went for your run? Did you leave the gate open when you left? Did you see anyone else by the back gate when you left?

The postwoman – Why were you delivering mail on a Sunday? What were you doing by the back gate of the Hound property? What made you think Mr Thorn was about to commit a crime?

Mr Thorn – Why were you walking past the property on Sunday morning? Why did you stop at the gate? Why did you look over your shoulder?

8–9 Personal responses will vary.

Unit 5

Pages 24-25: Mathematics – Statistics and Probability

1 H

2 c

3 Responses will vary.

Pages 26-27: HASS – History

1 c

2 d

3 Responses will vary and can include: being just and fair, honest, brave, inquisitive, patient, resilient, optimistic, a risk-taker, organised, independent, creative.

4 a

5 Responses will vary but may include that the Aboriginal people have a connection to place and have a very strong sense of connection to their ancestral lands. They are important elements of their history and culture. https://education.abc.net.au/home#!/media/152132/noongar-people-speak-about-a-sense-of-place

6 Uncle's account tells of the ghost-like men and their strange beasts coming into their land and how Uncle's people did not want them to stay but to move on. They were ghost-like because of the colour of their skin, pale like ghosts.

7 Personal responses will vary.

CRITICAL & CREATIVE THINKING CAPABILITY ASSESSMENTS

Inquiring, exploring & organising information & ideas assessments

Page 28: Pose questions

1 Responses will vary and can include: The farmer – What effect have the foxes had on your farm and on your ability to make money from your chickens? The fox – Why did you go to the farm when you knew it was so dangerous? The chicken – Since you knew a fox was in the area, how were you so unprepared for his attack?

2 Responses will vary and can include: The police officer may have turned to crime to make money./They may be infatuated with diamonds and can't help themselves to steal them./They have an inside knowledge on how to rob a store and leave no evidence./They wanted to test their skills to see if they could get away with the crime for excitement.

3 Responses will vary and can include the following: When did the robberies occur?/ Where were these stores located? Are they in one area?/What type of goods were stolen?/How did the thief leave no evidence? What did they do?/Who were the people who knew where the diamonds were kept in the store after closing time?/Why do the police have no suspects at all so far?

Page 29: Identify and clarify information and ideas

4 & 5 Personal responses will vary.

Organise and process information

6 Personal responses will vary.

Generating ideas, possibilities & actions

Page 30: Imagine possibilities and connect ideas

1 Responses may include: They would have feelings of fear and confusion./They may be worried about what will happen to them and be uncomfortable and concerned about the journey on board the ship.

2 Responses may include: Informing the judge that his decision to send John to prison meant that John stayed in a prison ship for three years before being transported./ The conditions must have been terrible, and he must have suffered loneliness and fear in that time./Inform the judge of John's early death in the colony and how he was harshly treated./Perhaps there was a better alternative than transportation and being freed to be influenced and used by organised thieves in London.

Consider alternatives

3 Personal responses will vary.

Page 31:

4 Responses may include: Healthcare workers because they have supported the community through tough times./Firefighters, as they saved the environment from bushfires./Scientists working on finding a solution to the plastic problem./Elon Musk for crewed missions to Mars.

Seek solutions and put ideas into action

5 Responses may include: Trading of services, for example one person could mow your lawn if you cleaned their family car./Followers on an online account/Virtual money/ Food items like chocolate/Clean water/Bottles of clean air/Ownership of parts of the moon or Mars/Seeds of vegetables and fruit.

6 Personal responses will vary.

Reflecting on thinking & processes

Page 32: Think about thinking (metacognition)

1 Responses may include: No-one had landed on the moon before, so no-one knew what was on the moon./The average person did not have access to telescopes to see what the moon looked like./Technology was not advanced enough to give scientists answers to life on the moon or what life could look like on the moon./Fake news was not something people living back then were familiar with, and questioning what they read was not a common practice.

2 Responses may include: Landings on the moon have already happened and people know the animals described in the article were not on the moon./Technology has advanced to make pictures of the moon readily available./People know more about the moon today and know there is not an atmosphere to support the large animals described./Fake news is a more common event and people today could be more likely to check the facts through Google and question the text.

3 Responses may include: Good idea – It attracted more people to read the paper./It created an interest in science./It was a bit of fun./The paper made money out of the series of stories. Not a good idea – It was fake news and people were lied to./People could become angry at being fooled and stop buying the paper which would mean the paper would eventually lose money./People do not like being tricked and it could result in a lawsuit./People may not believe anything the paper prints in future, even if it is true.

Page 33: Reflect on processes

4 i. Yes. Although the dog would be uncomfortable, the process is necessary for the wound to heal. ii. Some people may not think that two years of inconvenience (the means) is worth the stunning smile (the ends). However, many would think the process is worth the result. iii. No. This could be considered cheating which is not a good way to get what you want. iv. No. This action will certainly give you the largest piece of cake, but it involves lying which is not a good habit to form. v. Answers may vary and include that this is a quick fix for the problem and may work in the short term. However, this is not a good solution all the time. vi. Answers may vary and include that if dad knows about this and doesn't mind, then it could be okay. However, if you are deceiving dad and just being selfish, this is not okay. The means (deceit) did not justify the ends (having the chocolates you like).

Analysing, synthesising & evaluating reasoning & procedures

Page 34: Apply logic and reasoning

1 A red herring is a clue or piece of information which is misleading or distracting. (Don't be distracted by another definition, a dried herring, which turns red when it is smoked.)

2

Red Herring – not useful information	Useful information
1 A neighbour reported hearing Mrs Hound yell out, 'What are you doing, Chris?'	Henry is a rare and expensive breed.
2 A local postwoman said she was delivering mail at the time on a Sunday. (No mail is delivered on Sundays.)	Mrs Pug breeds and sells afghan hounds and other rare dog breeds.
3 Christine Rettel said Mr Chris Thorn was lurking near the open back gate in a slow and sneaky fashion.	Mr Thorn had said that Mrs Pug looked like her afghan hounds – check Mrs Pug's mugshot.

Page 35: Draw conclusions and design a course of action

3 Responses will vary.

4

Fact – can be proven	Opinion
• 100% natural ingredients • All Australian beef • Meets all your daily nutrition needs	• More than a meal • Homemade sauces like Grandma makes • The best burger in Australia • Your taste buds will love you. • You won't want fries with this one.

Evaluate procedures and outcomes

5 remembering, reliable, imagine, accurately, convicted, facial, innocent, decisions

ETHICAL UNDERSTANDING CAPABILITY

Unit 5

Page 37: Health & Physical Education – Personal, Social and Community Health

1 Responses may include: Evidence that the meeting takes place in the classroom is a poster on the wall/parent–teacher note/assignment with an F grade/adults are sitting on opposite sides of a desk/a teacher chair is in the picuture/file boxes in the background/the child is in school uniform.

2 Responses may include:

FRAME

1 – The father's arms are crossed, he's glaring, not smiling and looks angry. The girl has no eye contact to either adult, head down, not smiling and shoulders hunched. FRAME

2 – The father's speech bubble says he is disappointed, arched eyebrows, looking sideways and not smiling. The girl is looking down and away, her mouth turned down.

3 Responses may include: studying more, asking for help from the teacher or parents or friend.

4 Responses may include: movies, skating, bowling etc. The clues are choc tops, popcorn and drinks for sale. A girl is in uniform at a ticket booth and a sign, 'Kids 12 and under, half price' is displayed at the entrance.

5 Responses may include: FRAME 3 – The father is using his hand to hide what he is saying from the attendant. He is looking sideways and away. The girl is looking shocked with wide eyes and open mouth. The boy is looking sideways. FRAME 4 – The father is looking embarrassed and the girl is looking angry. The speech bubble has jagged edges to show anger.

6 Responses may include: FRAMES 1 & 2 – The girl is caught out for cheating/lying and the father is the one who is angry and disappointed. FRAMES 3 & 4 – The father is the one who is caught out cheating and the girl is angry at him for doing exactly what she did—cheat.

7 Responses may include: You're right, I shouldn't have done that. I'm glad you understand. Let's both promise not to cheat again.

Page 38: Health & Physical Education – Personal, Social and Community Health & Movement and Physical Activity

1 Personal responses will vary.

Pages 39-40: English – Literacy / Science – Science Inquiry Skills

1 National Aeronautics and Space Administration

2 b

3 Personal responses will vary.

4 A real event is something that actually happened and there is evidence to support this while a hoax is something done to trick people into believing or accepting as true something that is false.

5 Responses will vary but may include:

Information that supports the landing was a hoax	Information that supports the landing was real
• evidence on the film footage and photos of the landing, e.g., a mysterious letter C visible on a moon rock • odd markings on some of the photos given to the media, which looked like they had been taken on Earth, not the moon • Why is the flag fluttering on the 'moon'? • Who was filming the landing? • Why are there no stars in the sky?	• NASA is a government scientific group • original film footage and photos • interviews with the astronauts on Apollo 11 • moon rock and soil samples collected on the mission

6 Personal responses will vary.

Page 42: English – Literacy

1–2 Personal responses will vary.

Unit 6

Pages 43-44: English – Language / The Arts – Media Arts

1 b

2 d

3 Responses may include: The cat was found wandering alone on the footpath and wasn't hiding./It was too young to be on its own./It was used to human contact and was not a wild cat.

4 The girl is holding a bowl and cat carrier.

5 The girls' facial expressions are angry./The speech bubble is jagged./One girl is grabbing the other girl who is turned away.

6 Responses may include: Good idea: Both girls can have the cat for equal time./The idea will share the cost of keeping a cat./The cat will have two homes, not just one. Bad idea: Six months is too long in one house and the cat may not want to go to the other house./The girls may lose interest in the cat while waiting./The cat may not treat both houses as home./One girl will miss out on the cute kitten phase.

7 c

8 d

9 Personal responses will vary.

Pages 45-46: Health & Physical Education – Personal, Social and Community Health

1 e

2 d

3 Responses will vary and may include: You must never give out personal information online./You never agree to meet someone you meet online./You never send a photo of yourself to someone who is not a trusted friend or family member.

4 Responses may include: Tell a trusted adult./Log out of that site./Block the person asking.

5 Responses may include: A photo can give clues to where you live or school you attend. It will identify you. The image can be shared or used without your consent.

6 Responses may include: Tell Jo to tell a trusted adult and block the gamer who asked for the information.

7 Personal responses will vary.

ANSWERS

Pages 47-48: Mathematics – Number and Algebra

1

a	b	c	d	e	f	g	h	i	j	k	l	m	n	o	p	q	r	s	t	u	v	w	x	y	z
3	7	4	1	5	8	15	6	10	12	35	2	52	11	36	90	50	0	14	9	11/12	280	180	20	16	13

Delete this message after reading. It's on!!!!!!!!

Meet at the drinking taps after assembly. Mojo has water balloons – 4 each.

Fill the balloons and head to the library, top floor near the open walkway.

Wait for the bell. When the kids come out – attack! Then clear out! It will be so fun. Chrispie.

2 Chrispie's plan was to water bomb the students after assembly. Mojo was supplying the balloons—four each—and they were to meet at the top floor walkway by the library.

3 Responses will vary. Points for the plan could include: It would be fun./It would liven the day./It would be teamwork./It could be a way to gain popularity with students./ It's not messy as it is only water./It is not aimed at anyone in particular./It would be exciting. Points against could include: It may hurt someone from the height that they are dropped, especially if it is a younger student./You could get into very serious trouble with teachers./You may hit teachers or parents and not students./You will leave lots of litter with the burst balloons./It would not set a good example to younger students.

4 Personal responses will vary.

Unit 7

Page 49-50: English – Language & Literature

1 Responses may include: Cause – The character overslept. Action – He missed breakfast. Result – Because of this, he felt hungry. Possible action – He was thinking about taking part of Kookie's lunch. Possible consequences – He won't feel hungry./He will anger a friend./He may deprive her of lunch and she will feel hungry./He may get into trouble for stealing.

2 Responses may include: Make lunch the night before./Set an alarm to get up./Go to bed earlier./Keep the curtains open to let the light in, in the morning./Don't have a TV or device in the bedroom so as to get a good nights' sleep.

3 e

4 Personal responses will vary.

5 Personal responses will vary.

ANSWERS

Page 51: HASS – Civics and Citizenship

1 Responses will vary and may include:

RIGHT	RESPONSIBILITY
(Article 28) If children have the right to be educated …	then children also have the responsibility to attend school and engage with their learning.
(Article 13) If children have the right to get and share information ….	then children also have the responsibility to not harm others with this information.
(Article 24) If children have the right to good quality health care, clean water, nutritious food, and a clean environment to stay heathy …	then children also have the responsibility to stay safe and healthy and to help keep the environment healthy.

2 Responses will vary and may include:

RIGHT	RESPONSIBILITY
If you have been given the right to use a device in the classroom …	then you also have the responsibility to use it appropriately and obey the rules that go with its use.
If you have been given the right to join a sporting team …	then you also have the responsibility to attend training, turn up to games when expected and to play fairly.
If you have been given the right to have a sleepover at a friend's house …	then you also have the responsibility to obey the rules of that house and to respect the property and people in the house.

Pages 52-53: Health & Physical Education – Personal, Social and Community Health

1 What is happening? The new kid is being bullied by a group of friends. You are handed an item from the new kid's lunch box and are expected to eat it and go along with your friend's behaviour. How are you feeling? Responses may include: feeling confused, guilty, feeling sorry for the new kid, anger at the friend's behaviour, not wanting to be there, may be enjoying the scene. How is the owner of the lunch box feeling? Responses may include: scared, angry, embarrassed, confused, sad, accept the situation as it always happens to that kid.

TARGETING GENERAL CAPABILITIES: CRITICAL & CREATIVE THINKING AND ETHICAL UNDERSTANDING YEARS 5-6 © PASCAL PRESS ISBN: 978-1-925726-251

All the possibilities. Responses may include:

Possible solution	Consequences for this action	Possible feeling people may have after this action
1 Go along with the group.	• The group may get into trouble. • The new kid will go hungry. • The new kid will continue to be bullied. • You become a bully.	• The group may feel they have power over the new kid. • The new kid will feel sad and angry. • You could feel guilty and pity for the new kid.
2 Stand up to the group and say no.	• The group will turn on you and bully you. • You will lose your friends. • Others in the group may agree with you. • The new kid will be left alone by the group.	• The group may be angry with you. • The new kid may feel relieved. • You may feel proud of your actions or scared about the group's reaction.
3 Leave the situation and tell an adult.	• The group will turn on you and bully you. • You will lose your friends. • The bullying will stop for the new kid.	• You could feel proud of your action. • The group may feel betrayed by you and be angry at you. • The new kid may feel embarrassed by the whole incident. • Adults may feel disappointed in the behaviour of the group.

Bound into action. Personal responses will vary.

2 Responses may include: a, b, d

Page 54: Technologies – Design and Technologies

1 & 2 Personal responses will vary.

ETHICAL UNDERSTANDING ASSESSMENTS

Understanding ethical concepts & issues

Page 55: Recognise ethical concepts

1 & 2 Personal responses will vary.

3 Responses will vary and may include: A liar will need to remember all the lies that come from the first lie.

4 Personal answers will vary.

5 Personal responses will vary and you may like to discuss these with an adult: a True b True c Responses will vary. d Responses will vary. e Responses will vary. f False g True, for example, if I said to Leo, 'I can't go with you to the pool as I am going to the pictures with Alice.' You may be going to the pictures but not at the same time that Leo wants you to go to the pool.

Page 56: Explore ethical concepts in context

6 Responses will vary.

Reasoning in decision-making & actions

Page 57: Reason and make ethical decisions

1 Responses may include: go and play and get up early the next morning to complete work/negotiate with your parents/do some of the work and then go over to play/stay home.

2 Solomon, wisdom of Solomon, judgement of Solomon, cutting the baby in half, split the baby, you can't split the baby

Page 58: Consider consequences

3 Responses may include: Issue of safety. The parent in the cartoon does not know the other parents, so she does not know the house, the rules that will be in place and how many other students will be involved.

4 Responses may include: Julia's parents may know the other parents./They may not be as strict with their rules on sleepovers./They may live next door and are close at hand./They may want Julia to meet new friends.

5 Responses may include: There would be no boundaries for children to live by so they may not feel safe and secure./Children will not know what is expected of them./There would be no self-discipline and guidance in making healthy choices./Following rules is an important life skill that would be missed.

Reflect on ethical action

6 Responses may include rules for bedtime, bath time/hygiene, meals, homework, chores, screen time and sleepovers.

7 Responses will depend on the code devised.

TARGETING GENERAL CAPABILITIES: CRITICAL & CREATIVE THINKING AND ETHICAL UNDERSTANDING YEARS 5-6 © PASCAL PRESS ISBN: 978-1-925726-251

Exploring values, rights & responsibilities

Page 59: Examine values and consider points of view

1

DEFINE THE PROBLEM	
What is happening?	You want to go to the school camp, but you are worried that you may have chickenpox. This could mean you miss out on the camp that you have been looking forward to.
How are you feeling?	You are excited about the camp; however, you are worried and perhaps confused about the sores on your arm.

ALL THE POSSIBILITIES		
Possible solution	Consequences for this action	Possible feeling people may have after this action
1 You show your arm to your parents.	• You may find out you do not have chickenpox. • You may have to stay home. • You miss out on camp. • Your parents do not have to collect you from camp.	• You will be disappointed if you do not go. • Your parents may be relieved that they found out early and did not have to pick you up from camp. • Camp organisers, other students and their parents will be grateful you did not attend and pass on your infection.
2 You do not say anything to your parents.	• You infect others at the camp. • The camp may have to be shut down for quarantine and cleaning. • Your parents may have to come to collect you. • You do not get to do any of the activities. • You are not the only one affected by your decision, everyone is affected. • Your parents get into trouble from the camp organisers for sending you.	• You will be happy that you are on camp. • You will be disappointed if you fall ill during the camp and miss out on the activities. • Your parents will be annoyed if they find out you had symptoms of chickenpox before you left. • Classmates, their parents and the camp organisers may be angry with you for attending camp while you were infectious. • You could have easily passed on the disease to others.
3 Another solution you can think of	Personal responses will vary.	Personal responses will vary.

BOUND INTO ACTION	
What is your best solution?	Why did you choose this solution?
Personal responses will vary.	Personal responses will vary.

Page 60: Explore rights and responsibilities

1–3 Personal responses will vary.

ANSWERS

Targeting General Capabilities
CRITICAL & CREATIVE THINKING AND ETHICAL UNDERSTANDING

Years 5 & 6

ISBN: 978-1-925726-251

Published by Pascal Press
PO Box 250
Glebe NSW 2037
www.pascalpress.com.au
contact@pascalpress.com.au

Authors: Margaret Bishop and Susan Wilson
Publisher: Lynn Dickinson
Editor: Marie Theodore
Typesetter/Designer: Stacey Grainger
Illustrator: Paul Lennon

Printed in South Korea by Prinpia Co. Ltd.